EMBRACE ABUNDANCE

Also by Danette May

The Rise

Available at your local bookstore, or may be ordered by visiting:

Hay House USA: www.hayhouse.com®
Hay House Australia: www.hayhouse.com.au
Hay House UK: www.hayhouse.co.uk
Hay House India: www.hayhouse.co.in

EMBRACE ABUNDANCE

A Proven Path to Better Health, More Wealth, and Deeply Fulfilling Relationships

DANETTE MAY

HAY HOUSE, INC.

Carlsbad, California • New York City

London • Sydney • New Delhi

Scripture taken from the New King James Version®. Copyright © 1982 by Thomas Nelson. Used by permission. All rights reserved.

Published in the United States by: Hay House, Inc.: www.hayhouse.com® • *Published in Australia by:* Hay House Australia Pty. Ltd.: www.hayhouse .com.au • *Published in the United Kingdom by:* Hay House UK, Ltd.: www.hayhouse.co.uk • *Published in India by:* Hay House Publishers India: www.hayhouse.co.in

Cover design: Micah Kandros
Interior design: Claudine Mansour Design

Cataloging-in-Publication Data is on file at the Library of Congress

Hardcover ISBN: 978-1-4019-6150-3
E-book ISBN: 978-1-4019-6151-0
Audiobook ISBN: 978-1-4019-6152-7

10 9 8 7 6 5 4 3 2 1
1st edition, September 2021
Printed in the United States of America

This book is dedicated to all the
brave souls who are willing to look at the life they
are living and ask if they were made for more.
To the souls who are willing to release old stories
that have kept them separated from humanity,
Mother Earth, and the true essence of themselves.
To you, who will take these truths, embody them,
and live in your truest, fullest expression.

contents

let's begin

Having abundance is so much richer and deeper than what's in your bank account, the car you drive, the shoes you wear, or the home you live in. It is knowing that you are a divine being with a divine mission and divine connections. It's knowing that some of the best things in life are true friends whom you can lean on and pee your pants laughing with. It means living in a body that is operating at its peak state. It's feeling confident with your lover between the sheets. It's being free to be you and feel and express what is arising in all your dimensions. It's understanding that our children are our greatest assets and the legacy we leave to the world. It's operating in the knowing that you are meant to be financially free and serving your passion as the boldest, truest you. It's the peace of a calm mind with the inner knowing that you are known, loved, seen, and meant to be here.

As Florence Scovel Shinn said, "There is a place that you are to fill and no one else can fill, something you are to do, which no one else can do."

Through these pages, you will discover your ability to harness this deep truth: you are made for more and have within you the ability to create an abundant life. This is your destiny, and you can reach it through the infinite intelligence you carry within you.

The journey I have been on has at times had me feeling like I was lost in the wilderness, questioning my worth and pondering why I am here and what I am truly made of. I have made it my mission to understand the deeper realms of my existence, the power of my mind and spirit to co-create magic. I have worked with millions of people, helping them uncover the fullest expression of who they are. I've helped them transform their physical, mental, emotional, and spiritual lives by guiding them through healing movements to find a healing mind. And in doing this work, I have learned the magnificence that lies in each one of us. I have discovered how our minds, our internal frequency through our thoughts and feelings, mixed with our daily actions over time is the secret serum in bringing abundance to all areas of our life—creating a life that dreams are made of.

I have turned my mess into my message. The tools outlined in these pages helped me go from having a mere $47 to my name to now running two businesses generating eight figures each. I am living my purpose by helping others live their healthiest, most magnetic lives. I was a single mother who struggled with trust in partnerships, but I have since attracted my soul partner, who also happens to be my business partner. I went from having no close friends to loving my deep, inspiring, fun friendships. I feel closer to my children and feel closer to my creator.

Some of us are filled with fear and feel somewhat lost—about our health, mortality, finances, relationships, and governments. We are looking for hope, for a sign, for actions we can take to create more peace and abundance in all areas of our lives. What I know to be true, not only from my personal life but from listening to those who have come before us and the greats who live among us, is that regardless of what is happening outside us, we can control the world we create inside ourselves. And the world we create inside ourselves will be the reflection we see externally.

We shift things internally through the power of visualization. By getting into stillness, quiet, and communing with nature and a higher power, we can change our existence on a physical level.

My intention with this book is to provide you with these truths and a clear, concise road map to creating magic, bliss, and happiness in all areas of your life. I want to help you remember how to harness the infinite intelligence within you. I want to share with you the abundance actions that have shifted my life, the lives of my clients, and the lives of those who have come before us—that can now shift your life. I will guide you through simple actions you can do every day to start making significant changes in your life. The exercises in this book may seem small and simple, but as the saying goes, "By small and simple things are great things brought to pass."

In each section, you will hear a story about a successful entrepreneur, healer, or leader; an inspirational story from everyday life; or a myth or folktale. I will share a story from my own experience, and then provide you with a proven daily action that you can use right away to start living your abundant, beautifully divine life.

Collectively, these exercises nurture self-love and self-worth, which are the direct conduits that allow for more abundance in all areas of your life. We want to not only create a habit but tap into our subconscious minds to create lasting physical and spiritual change. These daily abundance actions will help you to turn feelings of:

anger into love
fear into faith
unworthiness into worthiness
being unheard into being heard
uncertainty into knowing
judgment into curiosity
separation into oneness

This is the time to look at your thoughts, the beliefs you boldly proclaim, and the actions you implement—and to be brave enough to question them. You hold the pen, you hold the paintbrush, and you hold the story that's going to be written. Let's start writing today.

abundance markers

The Ancestral Puebloans inhabited the intersection of what are now Arizona, New Mexico, Colorado, and Utah from approximately A.D. 100 to 1600, and they built their homes high in red rock cliffs or on sheer ledges. When I went to visit the cliffs in Arizona, I was feeling adventurous, and rather than use the obvious trails, I wanted to find my own way. I had heard that further exploration could be met with an untouched remembrance of the people who lived there and the energy they left behind in their homes—the remnants of bowls for grinding and their handprints on the walls.

As I inched my way around the cliff with my face buried against the rock, doing my best *not* to look at the 100-foot sheer drop just behind my heels, my heart did a somersault. Ahead of me was sheer red rock with no handholds. Behind me was a cliff covered with razor-sharp cactus. I frantically searched for something, anything I could use to get out of this situation. I inhaled deeply and looked intently at the cliff above me, and then I saw it: an ahu.

Hikers often use the term *ahu* to refer to a stack of rocks created by someone who has been there before you who marked the path to let the next traveler know that they are going the right way and that this is the next best step.

This tower of rocks gave me hope. It let me know that I wasn't alone on my climb. If I followed its suggestion and veered slightly to the left, I would find a safer, more efficient path to what I sought. With effort, as well as fear, exhaustion, and lots of scraped skin, I was able to head in the direction of the ahu. It led me to the ruins and the feeling of victory that only comes when you know you didn't give up and were divinely guided.

This book provides the ahus for a path of peace, purpose, and prosperity. As you go through this book, each section will end with this sign:

Each ahu marks what I call an abundance action, or a small step you can take to move closer toward the abundant life you deserve. You have worth. Remember your power, your mission, and your truth, and let them lead you to your innate abundance.

SELF-LOVE

noun. an appreciation of one's own worth or virtue; proper regard for and attention to one's own happiness or well-being

golden buddha

❧

Within you is the light of a thousand suns.

— ROBERT ADAMS

Every year, millions of people go to Thailand to see the Golden Buddha and to worship at his feet. This statue is almost 10 feet tall, and the gold that forms it is estimated to be worth $250 million. And it was lost for 200 years.

Before the Burmese Army invaded what was then Siam, Siamese monks swore to protect their beloved shrine. So they covered the Golden Buddha with clay 12 inches thick until it looked like nothing at all—just a cheap village shrine. And when the Burmese Army swept in, they did indeed pass it by. But the monks were slaughtered, and the Golden Buddha was lost, hidden in its clay disguise, and so it remained for two centuries.

The well-kept secret of the Golden Buddha remained intact until one day in 1955. A monastery needed to be relocated to make room for a new highway, as did the large clay Buddha from their temple. When the crane went to lift the statue, the weight was so tremendous that it began to crack. And just then the rain began to fall. The head monk was very concerned about damaging the sacred Buddha, so he ordered the crane to lower it back down to the ground. They then covered the giant idol with a tarp. Later that evening the head monk went to check on the Buddha. He took his flashlight and shone it into a crack in the clay, and to his surprise, he saw a glimmer of gold. As he took a closer look, he wondered if there was more beneath the clay. Using a chisel and hammer, he began the long process of knocking off shards of clay. The little gleam grew bigger and brighter until the extraordinary solid-gold Buddha that had been lost for so long stood before him. The beautiful Golden Buddha had been there all along!

CANNING VEGETABLES

We are all like the Golden Buddha. When we are born, we are pure, intuitive, and golden, and we shine with light. As we grow, we throw on layers of stories from other people's ideas, we buy into the belief that we are broken, we doubt our intuitive hits, and we start to cover up the light that is within us. We buy products and inject ourselves to feel prettier and worthier. We speak quietly and don't voice our opinions and beliefs so as not to disappoint those around us. We buy the shoes and the cars we believe we should want, and we pursue the friendships we think we need to make us feel valid. We allow negative emotions like anger, resentment, doubt, and fear to hide our true nature, even from ourselves.

We are so laden with clay, we have forgotten our Golden Buddha underneath.

I grew up in a lineage of women who believed that being a good mom meant working in the kitchen, making three meals a day, and canning food by taking fruits and vegetables from the garden, spending hours over the stove stewing them, putting them into mason jars, sealing the lids, and storing them for a rainy day. A good mother didn't work outside the home. Her priority was her children, the food, the cleaning, and ensuring there were vacuum lines in the carpet.

But my soul hates canning. Cooking elaborate, Martha Stewart meals and keeping organized are skills that are so out of reach for me that even after diligently applying the principles of *The Life-Changing Magic of Tidying Up*, I could still see Marie Kondo shudder every time I opened my kitchen drawer.

My soul asks for me to write my messy truth in books, to put on large events even if my knees are knocking. I feel pulled to stay up late at night researching ancient nutrition, mixing elixirs in my kitchen, and experimenting with superfoods. I yearn to walk the forests and try new adventures while traveling the world. I am called to dive deeper and deeper into my joy, my passions, and my truth and let the old, untrue narrative fall away.

Every day I have to unlayer all my clay. "I don't have to can vegetables". . . one chip off. "I don't have to organize closets". . . one chip off. "I don't have to be a good cook". . . one chip off. "I don't have to go to PTA meetings". . . one chip off. And as I chip off more and more layers, I learn that I *am* a good mom.

There comes a time when our old beliefs and feelings no longer serve us, and we must begin to chip away at them to find our magnificence that has been there all along.

 ## ABUNDANCE ACTION

Let's start chipping at the clay hiding your internal shine. What you say to and about yourself creates your reality. Loving all your dimensions, accepting the shadows and the light, is courageous and necessary—it allows you to emerge and walk in the truth of who you are. When you write and declare your truth with your words, you shift the neurons in your brain, therefore shifting your reality.

Take out your journal and write:

> *I love myself, therefore* . . . and then write all the things you love, from the parts you hide to the parts you want to be seen.

For example:

> *I love myself, therefore I love my imperfections.*
> *I love myself, therefore I love the anxiety I am feeling.*
> *I love myself, therefore I love my ability to see the light in others.*
> *I love myself, therefore (fill in a new statement).*
> *I love myself, therefore (fill in another new statement).*

Keep writing until you have filled up an entire page.

Now take a few minutes to let these words seep into your cells with mirror work. Mirror affirmation is a powerful manifesting tool because the mirror reflects back to you the feelings you have about yourself. It makes you immediately aware of what you are resisting and where you are open and flowing. As you learn to do mirror work, you will become much more aware of the words you say and the things you do. You will learn to take care of yourself on a deeper level than you have done before. Stand face-to-face with your reflection. Look into your eyes. Really look into them until the outline of your face blurs and you see only the depths of your eyes. Do not be afraid. You are meeting the deepest, purest, most radiant part of yourself through the soul of your eyes. As you look into your eyes, say all the loving things your soul longs to hear. Declare the truth. Anoint yourself with the power of your own word. You are your biggest rescue. Become your own best friend.

LEARNING TO LOVE YOURSELF

The biggest roadblocks to success are our own self-talk and inner voices. To help you go deeper and step into your truth with more ease, I created a special mirror meditation that you can download for free here:

www.EmbraceAbundanceBook.com/resources

alignment
can be sticky

❧

"It's impossible," said pride.
"It's risky," said experience.
"It's pointless," said reason.
"Give it a try," whispered the heart.

— UNKNOWN

Joan of Arc was born in 1412 in a small town in northeast France. From an early age, she declared that she was receiving visions from God and could hear voices of different saints. At about 13 years old, an angel told her to lead the French in a battle against the English and take back her homeland from English rule—and then once she drove the English out, she was to take the king to be crowned at Reims. These voices and visions continued for several years, until one day, when she was 16 years old, she decided it was time to take action. With this knowing in her soul, she stepped into her messy, faith-filled truth, even though it wasn't how she thought her life would turn out. She left behind the idea of living a quiet, predictable life spinning wool.

She started by approaching local leaders to take her to see the king. As you might imagine, they dismissed her. Joan did not give up. In order to effectively lead and fight, she cut her hair, dressed like a man, and became an expert horse rider and a proficient fighter. She led a convoy of soldiers to defend a city under siege, and even after being wounded by an arrow, she continued, inspiring the troops to fight harder until the English retreated.

Joan was eventually captured and held prisoner by the English, who tried to prove that she was a religious heretic. They declared her guilty of heresy and burned her at the stake. She was only 19 years old when she died on May 30, 1431.

Joan knew her purpose, she followed her intuitive knowing, and the power of her visions compelled her to move beyond the stickiness of fear and act on her truth.

RITUALS

When I was working on my first book, *The Rise*, I was pretty overwhelmed. It was fast-tracked and I needed to write it in six weeks. *The Rise* was about my messy, deep-dark, haven't-told-anyone truths. I was scared of rejection and being fully seen every day while writing that book— and at the same time, I was mapping out my first-ever live event for 1,500 women and launching Cacao Bliss and our new superfood company, which required hiring new employees and training them. And I spent just about every night trying to keep myself from crying because my teenager was telling me I was not being a good mother because she couldn't find her socks or I didn't remember her cross-country meeting.

I have never felt more out of alignment than at that time in my life. I felt like I was stuck in a washing machine on the high spin cycle with extra soap.

And the worst part was that while I was feeling this way, I was teaching other women about how to be in the flow and the feel-good feeling. I felt like a fraud. I had a short fuse, I was anything but pleasant, and I felt like I was spinning in a million directions.

Despite my hectic days, I continued my daily rituals, including my nature walks, morning prayer, and journal writing, and in these moments, I was able to find peace. And more than that, I found the certainty that, despite all the mess and uneasiness I was experiencing, I was right where I needed to be. Life was moving just as it was supposed to in its messy, raw, real unlayering way.

I learned that it was my *perception* of each activity, each demand for my time and attention, that determined whether it was sticky and hard, or easy and in flow. Was I a bad mother, or was my daughter just being a teenager? Was I a fraud, or was I just living my own messy truth? Was I going to screw up this new company, or was I fully guided and capable?

When I thought about each of the tasks I was called to do—write the book, put on the event, get the superfoods out into the world, stay up extra late to lie by my girls and hear them talk about their day—even though I was so tired I just wanted to curl up in my blankets and shut down the day, I knew that each of these tasks was a part of my truth. I was doing what my inner being was asking me to do.

And the stickiness didn't last. All those things that felt so difficult became easier once I got used to them.

Alignment means "aligned with your truth." You have permission to feel all the emotions—angry, sad, happy, elated, excited, terrified, questioning, knowing, powerful, and unequipped—and still be in alignment. You have permission to change your mind and your beliefs every second of every day and still be truthful.

When we are aligned with the truth of who we are, our life begins to flow. It's when you stop being positive for the sake of being positive and start being *you* that you find your alignment.

ABUNDANCE ACTION

Even when our life is going just as we planned and dreamed, it can still feel unsteady at times. You can be in alignment and not *feel* like it. Not all aligned actions feel like flow, like life is easy and everything is moving smoothly. The way to figure it out is to get quiet and check in with yourself.

Are you living in your truth? Are you moving in the direction that your heart is asking you to move? Are you making decisions not because they feel easy or hard but because they feel *right*?

The stories you tell yourself about that unsteadiness, that stickiness, can affect your alignment. So what are you saying to yourself about your current situation? Can you choose to create a new narrative, one that will support you? If you find yourself in the stickiness and discomfort of rising into your soul's path, try to steady yourself by doing the following every day:

1. Say and feel into these words: "I choose to feel good." We must decide and declare.

2. Notice and become aware of the words you are speaking or feeling. Awareness is huge. In your awareness you can laugh at the false stories you are telling yourself and create a new story. This takes skill, but once you start the practice of writing a new, supportive story, you can stop your negative thoughts in their tracks. This skill can take your life on a magic carpet ride.

3. Forgive yourself for your misaligned thoughts and actions. We are all human, and this is part of our growth. When we forgive and offer grace, we can begin to expand into the art of getting out of our way and letting a higher power take the lead.

the door

Change the way you look at things,
and the things you look at change.

— Dr. Wayne Dyer

There was once a man who had committed a crime. The law of the land said that he had two choices: he could serve his sentence in prison, never to breathe free air again . . . or he could face the door.

Nobody knew what was behind the door. It was deep in the castle dungeons, and people speculated that it contained venomous snakes, dragons, and even hydras, but no one knew for certain. All they knew was that whatever it was, it was worse than they thought.

The criminal quickly chose prison. As he was being taken to his cell, he asked the guard, "So, out of curiosity, what's behind the door? I'm obviously never going to get out of here to tell anyone."

The guard paused. "Freedom," he said at last. "That door leads outside. It's how we go home every night. But no one has ever taken it. Everyone is so afraid of the unknown that they always choose to lock themselves away."

PEACE

Most divorces are unpleasant, and mine was no exception. I was driving in the city, which even on a normal, high-vibe day is a monumental task. I am a country girl through and through. I live in the country for several reasons: no stoplights, no ridiculous traffic, fewer people, and the hermit lifestyle. On this particular day, I was picking up a few things that I could only find in the city, driving in the second lane of a four-lane road, and out of nowhere, I felt my chest tighten up and breath shorten. At first I wondered if I was having a heart attack. I knew I had to pull over to the side, which only created feelings of being suffocated in the car in the middle of traffic. My breathing became raspy, and it was hard to catch some air. I dug in deeper to focus harder to get my car pulled over.

Once I was on the shoulder, my body released. I Could. Not. Breathe. Which made me panic even more. I called my best friend, and between sobs I managed to say, "I can't breathe. I think something is wrong with me. I just want you to know where I am in case I'm having a heart attack."

My friend asked me what I was feeling, and once I shared, she said, "Honey, you are not having a stroke or heart attack. You are having an anxiety attack."

"How is that possible? I wasn't thinking about anything that was wrong in that moment. Nothing is wrong."

"Anxiety attacks come out of nowhere at times," my friend explained. "Take a minute and just breathe with me. Now ask your anxiety what it is trying to tell you."

"It says I have been so busy trying to not feel the pain of the divorce and how truly scared I am." I paused, unable to continue.

"Go on," my friend urged. "How do you feel? Danette, you have to feel to heal. You have to stop trying to deflect by being so busy so you can feel. The body had a moment to feel because you are trapped in a car with yourself. Can you take a moment and just feel?"

Finally, I said, "I am scared I am ruining my children by dismantling their family. I am scared of what my ex will do to make my life miserable. I am terrified that I am turning my back on everything I ever said I believed in. My religion, my beliefs, my marriage, love, who I am and who I am not. I am afraid of being alone. I am afraid that I do not deserve true happiness." On and on, I kept expressing and feeling as my breaths became fuller and my chest opened up.

I had a right field and a left field of choices in front of me, and I wanted to be on a completely different field. One field was laden with stats on divorce and remarriage, finances after divorce, and the outcome of children from divorced parents. The other field proclaimed marriage should last until death do you part. This field said a good girl doesn't divorce the nice guy and hurt her children.

And then there was the field that I wanted to create. This field had no stats, no given outcomes, just the tuning-in to my gut. I had my instincts, my knowing, and the idea that I was made for more. I knew that my kids were made for more and that if I tuned in to my truth and my instincts, we would find our happiness.

ABUNDANCE ACTION

We will all be faced with overwhelm from time to time. It simply cannot be avoided—but we can mitigate its impact by creating a grounding routine, something that will support us as we are faced with the unknown. When we create rituals that honor us, we tell the Universe that we feel worthy of ease and peace in our lives. And when we show up for ourselves by making these choices, we get more of ease and peace in our lives.

This full morning ritual will take you approximately 15 to 20 minutes. It is a beautiful way to enter the day feeling steady, grounded, and connected. Morning rituals send a signal to your brain that you are worthy, and those who feel worthy are magnets for abundance. Try this morning routine for 10 days, feeling into its effects, and then adjust it as needed to make it a part of your life.

1. Upon waking, instead of making your usual coffee, which could be adding unnecessary anxiety through its caffeine content, try making this Cacao Bliss Elixir:

   Ingredients
   $^1/_2$ cup nut milk (almond, coconut, or oat)

   1 large scoop Cacao Bliss (available at http://embracecacao.com/), or 2 teaspoons raw cacao + 2 teaspoons raw

honey or coconut sugar + ¹/₄ teaspoon turmeric + ¹/₄ teaspoon cinnamon

1 additional teaspoon raw honey (optional)

Heat milk with ¹/₂ cup water until it is just steaming, and stir in the remaining ingredients. Raw cacao contains a chemical called anandamide, known as the "bliss molecule." This can help increase the feeling of love for self and others, as well as a sense of euphoria. The additional superfoods in the blend may work to increase energy, balance hormones, and decrease anxiety and brain fog.

2. Stretch for five minutes. Reach out and down to your toes, swaying from side to side, and exhale deeply.

3. Sit for 5 to 10 minutes in meditation or prayer. Close your eyes, and focus on breathing into your belly, filling it up with as much air as you can. Then slowly exhale all that air out through your mouth. Repeat 10 times. Thank your Heavenly Father (or Source, or the Universe) for this day you have been given. Express gratitude for your health, your body, and your ability to serve the people in your life. Mention

three or more things you are grateful for. Ask how you can show up as your highest self today. Ask for the courage to be loving, kind, and peaceful.

**Disclaimer: Consult your doctor
if you are experiencing severe anxiety or depression.*

words

❧

Whatever follows "I am"
will always come looking for you!

— JOEL OSTEEN

Ian Humphrey was born two months early. His mom went into labor when a woman poured boiling water over her, sending her tumbling down the stairs and leaving third-degree burns all over her body. She was unable to care for newborn Ian, so he went to live with various friends and relatives and was passed around for the first three years of his life.

At the age of three, he got into his mom's pain medication. He pulled it out of her purse, ate it all like candy, and went into a coma. Child Protective Services took him away from his mother and put him into the foster care system. He went to live with a woman called Miss Alexander. She would lock him in a closet and beat him. He was burned with a hot iron regularly, and he was sexually abused while in her care. She would open the closet door and stand over him, saying, "You're stupid. You're never going to amount to anything." And the most destructive part was Ian believed her.

Through grace, Ian's grandmother was able to get full custody, and she removed him from Miss Alexander's toxic care. Things got better, but then they got worse again. Ian's mother died when he was 12 years old, and when he was 19, he found himself standing in front of a judge. He was sentenced to 15 years in prison for armed robbery.

It felt like everything Miss Alexander had said about him had come true. And it wasn't even just Miss Alexander: no one in Ian's life had told him or had helped him believe that he could be or do anything worthy of love.

One day a man named Charles Lyles came to visit Ian in prison. Charles shared with him, "Prison doesn't have to be your life. You can get out of here, and you can do great things. I believe in you."

Hearing these words was a big deal to Ian. Charles didn't see as he was leaving, but Ian stared after him with tears running down his face. No one had ever said anything like that to Ian before, and Ian *believed* what he heard. Four years later, with belief and powerful words seeping through his cells, Ian walked out of that prison on parole. He returned to his grandmother's advice that she had given him from the time he was very young: be grateful for every single day. Finding something to be grateful for every day, whether it was large or small, helped him find his way through his trauma. Choosing empowering words, saying them and believing them, is how he made it to where he is today as a general manager of a successful multimillion-dollar company and a highly sought-after inspirational speaker.

Ian's story proves that words matter. The phrase "sticks and stones may break my bones, but words can never hurt me" is far from the truth—words have an immense power to harm. But they also have an immense power to heal. The words we speak can heal our bodies. They can lift our energy, rewire our neurological pathways, and heal our subconscious reprogramming. They can help regenerate our cells and organs, prevent oncoming disease that has been passed on in our DNA through suppressed emotions, and improve our lives.

EGGS

When I was five, I was at the grocery story with my mom and I was trying to be helpful. My little ole self wanted to feel significant and make my mom's day feel a little less burdensome. I knew eggs were on her list, so I walked over and grabbed a carton. But the lid slid open and a dozen eggs spilled onto the floor, creating a piece of art with clear slime and bright orange circles. My mom gasped while others looked with horror at the mess that now needed to be cleaned up.

"Oh no!" she exclaimed. "What have you done? You are so clumsy. Don't touch anything."

I seized these words, shoved them deep down inside, and let them drive me to a lifetime of caution, questioning my abilities and waiting for the fall.

Most of us have experiences like this in our past from imperfect parents, friends, and teachers. Most of us have done and said things out of hurt or shock to our children and others, causing a cycle of low self-worth. We are all imperfect humans, learning, growing, course-correcting, forgiving, and creating new pathways. My mother was a loving, caring mother and, like most of us, got caught up in the moment and said things she didn't really mean. In all likelihood, she has no memory of that moment. So why would I choose to continue carrying these beliefs that I am about to do something wrong when I am only trying to help and that I am someone who will mess things up?

Words have power, and once they are in our cells, we operate unconsciously, fulfilling the meaning we give them. It was up to me to release the hold of this memory and give it a new meaning.

The way you write a new story, a new feedback loop in your psyche, is to go back to the original scene in your mind. Really see it and feel into it, as if you are reliving it. See yourself carrying the eggs over to the cart. Feel your pride as you are about to do something right and helpful for your mom. Then see the lid pop open and the eggs spill out onto the floor.

Now here is where you create a *new* memory and feedback loop.

You see the people looking at you, but instead of feeling their disdain, you see them looking in surprise—just as you would as an adult if you saw a dozen eggs spill to the floor. Now see these people in complete understanding and relief that it wasn't them, as it would be so easy for this to happen to anyone, child or adult.

Now see your mom. She sees the eggs spill, and instead of gasping and saying hurtful things, she comes over and puts her arms around you. She says, "Thank you for trying to be so helpful. Don't worry; they're just eggs, and they will get cleaned up."

As healers of our own journey, we can form new neural pathways by replaying a different outcome over and over in our minds through visualization, intentionally uplifting our energy, and rewiring our neurological pathways, so we release the old, negative patterns that have been causing us to continue to attract these same feelings of unworthiness, fear, or frustration and re-create a story of power, significance, bravery, and success. The human mind is one of the most powerful tools we have. We are what we think. What we think, we become.

ABUNDANCE ACTION

We can rewire old patterns of pain and triggers so they do not keep manifesting in our life by going back to the scene, back to the moment when that disempowering story was created.

One time per week, close your eyes and set an intention to remember an earlier experience that caused you stress or pain and may still be challenging for you. Once you have identified an event or even multiple moments that you feel comfortable revisiting, visualize a more positive outcome, playing out the scene differently. If you do this, you will encourage more love, power, acceptance, and worth to enter your life.

FORGIVENESS FOR HEALING

Forgiveness is another powerful tool that can take you beyond past trauma. If you desire to discover the freedom that forgiveness can bring into your life, download and listen to this meditation for the next 7 to 10 days:

www.EmbraceAbundanceBook.com/resources

SPIRIT

*noun. the nonphysical part
of a person that is the seat of emotions
and character; the soul*

first you must decide

❧

Once you make a decision,
the universe conspires to make it happen.

— RALPH WALDO EMERSON

From 1940 to 1954, many runners were on the quest to break the four-minute mile. Athletes around the world trained hard with this one goal in mind. Roger Bannister, a junior doctor with a dream in his heart and minimal time to train, knew the power of writing something down, seeing it in his mind, and combining it with action. He took out a little piece of paper, wrote down *3.58*, and placed it in the bottom of his running shoe. Every time he ran, he would see that number in his mind and see himself breaking the four-minute barrier.

In 1954 Roger broke through the barrier, running a mile in just six-tenths of a second less than four minutes.

Once that seemingly impossible barrier was conquered, it felt like anyone could do it. Just 46 days after Bannister's race, an Australian runner named John Landy came in two seconds short of four minutes, and a year after that, three runners finished in under four minutes *in the same race*. Since then, thousands of runners have managed this feat.

Whether you think you can or think you can't,

you are right!

SEE IT

I grew up in a family of runners. My brothers and I competed in high school, and I ran in college, as well. As we have all gotten older and had children of our own, our children have also become runners. It's the main topic of conversation at any family gathering—who is running, how far, and in what meet? My oldest daughter, Sarah, was an exception. She had created a story that she wasn't a "true" runner like her mom, cousins, and uncles. And then in her sophomore year of high school, she decided to give cross-country a try.

Frankly, when she started out, she wasn't that good at it. Her legs felt heavy and out of shape, and she definitely wasn't fast—and that was okay! She ran for fun, and she felt good running with a team and trying a new sport.

And then one day during the summer before her junior year, Sarah told me, "I've decided that I am going to be a good runner. I'm not going to just be a good runner; I'm going to be one of the top runners. Will you support me in this?"

There was power in this statement. She *decided*, all on her own, with no teammates or coaches, or her mom telling her to—just with her own internal desire and guidance.

Over the next few months, I watched her transform into a more efficient runner. Sarah said, "I know I'm faster than I've been. I know that I'm doing really well in practices, but I have a hard time seeing myself winning. I can see myself getting third place or fourth place, maybe even second place, but I can't quite see getting first place."

My response to her was, "You have nothing to prove outside of yourself. Dreaming and trying and not succeeding doesn't make you any worse off than you are right now in this very moment. You have nothing to lose. You are not a failure if you give it your all, if you pour your heart and soul into it, and it doesn't happen. You keep dreaming, you keep feeling into it, seeing it, and trusting. That's your only job."

In her first meet of that season, Sarah ran five minutes faster than her best time the previous year, and she won! Over the course of that year, she became one of the top runners in the state of Colorado.

Our ability to visualize is our divine connection with Source. We can close our eyes and see and feel our desire. The problem is we're often afraid because we think, *If it doesn't happen as I see it and I go for it, will I be a failure?*

Just like Sarah's soul, your soul wants to dance in the vision of your desire. It wants to feel the joy of living out your truest, fullest expression. To become a magnet for your dreams, you must first decide what it is you choose. Be clear; declare it. And then once you've seen and felt it, you can let it go and trust—because it just happened. You felt it fully in your visualization.

ABUNDANCE ACTION

Take out a journal or a piece of paper and write down with clarity something you choose to bring into your awareness. Be mindful of your choice of words, for they hold magnetic power. Avoid the word *want*, as you will only get more wanting. Instead use words such as *I choose*, *I see*, *I have*, and *I am* as you begin your sentences. Keep this writing where you can see it. Every day, close your eyes and visualize or mentally rehearse that dream or desire, imagining it manifesting in your life. See yourself doing the very thing you desire. Feel it. What are you wearing? How does experiencing this dream feel in your body? What is happening around you? Feel the gratitude, excitement, and wonder as you witness and feel that very thing in your heart coming true.

There is power in deciding. There is power in belief. There is power in seeing your desire and feeling it as if it is already here.

SEE YOUR SUCCESS

The most successful people in the world almost universally credit visualization for the achievement of their goals. To help you experience the power of this in your own life, I created a special guided visualization, available to download *for free* at

www.EmbraceAbundanceBook.com/resources

holy hell yes

❧

If prayer is you talking to God,
then intuition is God talking to you.

— Dr. Wayne Dyer

Nelson Mandela, a social rights activist, politician, leader, and follower of intuition, was South Africa's first Black president. In his twenties he fought against apartheid (institutionalized racial segregation in South Africa), and when he joined the African National Congress, he led a campaign of peaceful protest against the South African government. In 1962 he was charged with treason for standing up to the apartheid and imprisoned for 27 years.

For the first 18 of those years, he was confined to a small cell without a bed or plumbing and was forced to do hard labor at a quarry. He was separated from his family to a cruel extent—he was allowed to write and receive a letter only once every six months and could meet with a single visitor once a year for a mere 30 minutes.

In 1985 Mandela was offered a conditional release from prison by the government, but only if he renounced "illegal activity." Doing so would betray his principles, his leadership, and the long struggles of his people. And so Mandela replied to this offer with, "What freedom am I being offered while the organization of the people remains banned? . . . What freedom am I being offered if I must ask permission to live in an urban area? . . . Only free men can negotiate. Prisoners cannot enter into contracts."

Mandela's decision to remain in prison drew attention to the issue. Mandela intuitively understood that his sacrifice was strategic and would help bring about political change. Five years later this man of deep principle was released without conditions. When he became president of South Africa, he instituted profound changes in his country. His nation was no longer ruled by a white minority, and Mandela navigated the challenging transition with great wisdom and discernment, as he saved his country from economic collapse and guaranteed the rights of that white minority, even after so many years of oppression.

DISCERNMENT

On my wedding day to my first husband, my sister-in-law and I were in a small hotel bathroom as she was doing my hair. With each twist of the hair, I felt safer and safer, and I blurted out, "I don't want to get married."

Sister-in-law: "What!? Why?"

Me: "I don't know. I have a bad feeling inside."

Sister-in-law: "Everyone feels nervous on their wedding day, and they question if they want to get married."

My mind raced. *What? Everyone feels this growing disturbance in their belly right before they are about to link arms and confess their love? They feel this rage and rumbling underneath the skin, hot, smoldering, and ready to erupt? Everyone feels like the runaway bride?* That day, I trusted my sister-in-law more than I trusted myself. I turned off my intuition and buckled down to live the story that was laid before me: Be a good wife. Don't feel too much. Have children as soon as possible. And do not ever question your marriage or the man in it again.

Discernment is derived from the Greek word *diakrisis*, which refers to a spiritual power that allows you to distinguish between the spirits that will cause harm and the spirits that will assist you. We get to discern when a phone call, an email, or a visit from a friend is going to add to our day, or if it won't be beneficial and will instead distract us from what we are meant to do for the higher good. We get to discern whether it's a good idea to allow our teenage child to go out with her friends at night. We can see whether a business deal that looks good on paper is not actually in our best interest.

Discernment is the difference between feeling led by the day, pulled this way and that, and *claiming the day* and ultimately your life.

Discernment is different from judgment. When we judge someone or ourselves, we include ideas of right or wrong, morality and immorality, about what should or should not be. When it comes to engaging with others, discernment is a vital tool. With discernment, we are taking account of the facts, feeling into our intuition and spidey senses, and making a decision based on them alone.

I have come a long way since that moment of getting dolled up in the bathroom for my big wedding day. We should never say yes to anything or anyone from a place of fear or obligation. Our soul's work is not to meet everyone else's expectations. It is to live our truth and answer only to the holy hell yeses of our life. That's where our freedom and our fullest, most authentic expression can be found.

 ## ABUNDANCE ACTION

On this path to your abundant, most expressed life, you will have choices to make. You will need to feel into what is your best next move. During these times, remember that you are not alone. There are divine guides, angels, and spirits all around you, waiting for you to simply get still and ask for their support. When you have a difficult decision to make and you choose to access your discernment, intuition, and knowing, the steps below will help you find the internal wisdom coursing through your veins.

1. Every day, get out in nature where you feel peaceful. It may be a walk on your street or sitting on the beach or at a park. Nature and its many forms of weather have healing neurons that not only heal your cells but open magnetic portals for information, wisdom, and clarity.

2. Close your eyes and feel the presence of your own stillness and breath.

3. Ask! Ask God, the Universe, Source, your
   guides, or whatever it is you believe in to give
   you clarity. Ask: *Is it a holy hell yes? Will it nour-*
   ish me, renew me, inspire me, or expand me? Is it
   within alignment of what my soul wants?

4. Be very aware that you will receive answers or
   signs. Pay attention so you see the signs when
   they present themselves. Signs can come in
   many forms: animals, plants, a surge of wind,
   a sound, or a conversation with another person. Notice the feelings that come up during
   conversations or experiences throughout the
   day. Holy hell yeses tend to feel warmer in the
   body. They feel like love. They can also feel like
   butterflies in your belly. Remind yourself that
   saying yes *only* to the holy hell yeses takes fine-
   tuned precision, and saying no takes faith.

unseen forces

❧

All the strength and force of
man come from his faith in things unseen.

— JAMES FREEMAN CLARKE

Harriet Tubman was in Dorchester County, Maryland, in the mid-1800s. Enslaved, she knew what working tirelessly for someone else meant and witnessed the abuse of family members and friends along with being abused herself. She knew this was not to be her life. She knew she was made for more and that every person should be free.

She traveled over 100 miles to find her freedom—not eating for days, coming up against wild animals and people chasing her, and having to cross a deep river when she didn't even know how to swim. She prevailed because she trusted in God to see her through.

And she didn't stop there. She leaned into the mission that was set before her and set free enslaved person after enslaved person—men, women, children, the elderly—sometimes leading them as far as 500 miles. And she succeeded because she remained fluid and connected to her intuitive knowing.

When Harriet was a child, she had sustained a brain injury that caused her to have seizures or fall asleep suddenly. When this happened, she received messages and warnings that came to her as profound visions. As a conductor of the Underground Railroad, she was navigating a complicated system and always had a plan for how she would travel to the North. When she received one of these visions, she altered the plan, obeying her intuition. If she was told to go a different route, she would. That willingness to bend and sway, to shift with what was being asked of her in each moment—even if it was not the plan—was her strength, and it helped ensure her success.

Thanks to her trust in her intuition, Harriet Tubman was never caught, and she freed over 300 enslaved people.

WALLS

I know that every person who has come before us lives within us. Their legacies course within our veins. We can learn from their examples and follow our inner guidance and our connection to divine power, remaining fluid and flexible in our approach.

As I built my businesses, raised my daughters as a single mother, and navigated a new marriage, I know that staying in my fluidity, staying open to the changes that come, and knowing that I would be able to navigate them, made all the difference in my success. I did this by committing to daily prayer every morning, by writing in my journal and asking, *What would you have me know?* and by finding stillness in nature so that I could hear wisdom from a higher power.

I carry a lot of masculine, or driving, energy. It drives the direction and vision of my business and family life, and it creates a structure. Yet this energy is not complete if I do not nurture and follow a feminine, or more intuitive, flow state. Even as I write this book, the masculine in me wants me to sit down in front of my computer at a designated time every day—whether I'm inspired or not. That's the driven, tactical, practical thing to do, and it will help me get this book written on time. The feminine, more graceful part of me knows better. It knows when I am typically most creative during the day, or when my kids most likely need my attention. My work flows and schedules around these times. This has often had me writing before 5 A.M. and breaking up my time to walk in the woods and receive inspiration.

I've held so many meetings while walking in nature, with millions of dollars on the line. The creative meetings at my company don't take place sitting around a table in a boardroom; instead my leadership team goes for hikes together or gathers on comfy couches with tea, cacao, or coffee in hand. When my business partner and I want to map out our three-year vision, instead of sitting with our computers in front of us, we hike to the top of a peak with a 360-degree vantage point. Removing the walls, the containers, the paradigms, the old, outdated belief systems, and the untruths gets me more connected to the greatest source of wisdom of all—Mother Nature. I let her speak the truth of what I need to hear.

ABUNDANCE ACTION

Every day, let Mother Nature help you get into more flow and lead you to more abundance. Nature is the greatest teacher of abundance. Every season, there is decay, renewal, and regrowth. Every part of nature—plants, soil, air, the sun—works synergistically together. Listen to nature, walk in her mountains, and feel your bare feet crunch on her ground. Place your hand on a tree, or, better yet, wrap your arms around it for a hug. Close your eyes and feel the tree's strength and unconditional love. Set an intention that you would like to draw closer to this energy and that you would love to receive deeper wisdom. Let Mother Earth know that you would love to flow more in faith, belief, and power. This moment is yours. It can be a prayer, an intention, or a stillness.

when life throws you curveballs, swing or duck

❦

*Always believe that
something wonderful is about to happen.*

— Dr. Sukhraj Dhillon

With hope comes faith; with faith come miracles. We have the power to be the driving force for the miracles in our own lives.

When my friend Amy was going to the workshop of her dreams she had been saving for, she had planned on arriving early and getting the best seat in the house. But as fate would have it, her flight was delayed, there was traffic, and when she finally made it to the event location, there was no parking. The parking attendant said, "Sorry, you're going to have to park a mile or so down the road and walk up."

It was raining. Amy was wearing her kick-ass heels. She didn't have an umbrella. This was *terrible*. She was so excited, and now she was going to be late, miss some of the conference, show up wet, and most likely not get a seat.

Amy wanted to break down and cry. She'd tried so hard to mitigate any chaos, and now she was feeling like the Universe was telling her to forget it; this workshop that was supposed to open up a new life path wasn't going to happen.

Just as she was beginning to spiral, Amy stopped. She leaned back from the feelings of frustration brewing inside her. She stopped trying to "fix" the situation, and she decided to trust. She set the intention that something would happen to make this work out for her. She decided to stay in a miracle mindset.

And then the parking attendant said, "Wait a minute. Actually, someone's leaving. You can take their spot right here near the entrance, where you won't get wet."

So Amy parked and raced into the workshop, and, of course, there were no seats left. But once again she took a breath. She leaned away from the panic and frustration she was feeling, and she trusted. She thought, *I intend that there will be an open seat.*

A gal in the front row saw her and waved. Amy went over, and the woman said, "You can take this seat, sweetie. The person who had been sitting here just took off."

LEAN AWAY

Some of my greatest, hardest work is mastering the art of leaning away from triggers and expecting a miracle. My triggers can come from seemingly random things, from trying to connect via Zoom for an important meeting and the tech deciding to go out to giving a presentation where I spill coffee on my shirt.

My intimate relationships can also be massive triggers. These triggers can take me from feeling on top of the world to spinning down a dark rabbit hole within seconds. The key is to be aware of the emotions I am feeling. If it feels off and at times downright frustrating, it's an indication that this is my moment to lean away and put into practice a miracle mindset, watching the Universe do her song and dance.

I saw this work in real time a couple years ago. Craig and I had attended Tony Robbins's Unleash the Power Within workshop. It was a four-day event, and there were around 8,000 people in attendance. If you've been to a Tony Robbins event, then you know the first day is all about raising your frequency, claiming that positive outlook to attract and manifest your dreams—staying in a "peak state." It was an incredible experience, and we ended that first day laughing, hugging strangers sitting next to us, and feeling this high of love and connection.

As you can imagine, the hotels in the area were completely sold out. The event started early in the morning on the first day, and so when it ended late in the evening, we all trooped over to our hotels at the same time to check in, exhausted but still super charged. Unfortunately the hotel Craig and I were checking into was not prepared for hundreds of people arriving all at the same time. The line to check in snaked out of the lobby and out into the street.

At first everyone was very patient, chatting with one another about the day's experiences and rolling in the aftermath of the high we had experienced at the event. However, once we'd been standing in line for about an hour, people began to get a little cranky. Some started to grumble, others tried to cut in line, there were a few altercations—it was getting ugly.

As Craig and I stood in that line waiting with everyone else, I thought, *What an interesting phenomenon. We've just come from a day of learning how to stay in a peak state and manifest miracles, and here we are with a prime opportunity to practice.*

So I took a minute and leaned back from the emotions I was feeling. I'm the queen of efficiency, and this whole situation was driving me up the wall. I also was tired and annoyed at the hotel. I leaned away from my negative emotions, becoming an observer versus feeling like I was in the middle of it, and set an intention. I intended that the hotel would open another line, and that we would move through that line quickly and get to our room and go to sleep.

Just five minutes after I set that intention, a member of the hotel staff came around the corner, looked straight at me, and said, "I'm going to help you guys. Let's start a new line right here."

I couldn't believe it! We got checked right in and hurried into the elevator and upstairs to get a decent night's sleep.

Every time I've leaned away from triggers, set an intention, and expected miracles, I have watched that miracle arrive. Abundance is on the other end of leaning away from agitation. Our frequency is more important than our strategy when it comes to our relationships, our businesses, and creating our dreams.

ABUNDANCE ACTION

When you are faced with a situation that creates a surge of triggers within you, try this process to get on your magic carpet ride of miracles and greater abundance:

1. **Be aware of your emotions.** You don't have to "fix" your emotions, much less a situation that feels out of your control. When you believe you have to fix your emotions, you are signaling to the Universe that something is wrong and you will receive more experiences that you feel you need to fix. There is nothing to fix. There is only observance of what is.

2. **Lean away from the negative emotions.** This involves taking a deep breath and seeing yourself and the situation as if you are out of your body and just observing what is happening. This will usually tip the anger and frustration scale down immediately. Remember that what you focus on will expand. If you are feeling rage, you will get more things to rage about. When you choose to look at your life from an eagle-eye perspective and see that everything is happening *for* you, your emotions will more easily neutralize, and you can redirect your energy to focus on what you truly desire.

3. **Set an intention.** Let the Universe know what you desire by making a request or setting an intention of what you would like to unfold. The Universe knows the greater good for all involved and may create a scenario that is somewhat different than you intended, but it will often be more than you even imagined or declared.

4. **Trust.** The miracle is coming. All you need to do is let it. As we stand in full belief and trust, we become a magnet for juicy blessings.

finding peace
in chaos

❧

Peace. It does not mean to be in a place
where there is no noise, trouble, or hard work.
It means to be in the midst of those
things and still be calm in your heart.

— UNKNOWN

Major Rhonda Cornum, a 34-year-old wife, mother, and
flight surgeon, had joined the military, biochemistry de-
gree in hand, as a way of serving her country and being
an example to her daughter of what strong women are
capable of. She was on a search and rescue mission at the
height of the Gulf War when her Black Hawk helicopter
was shot down by Iraqi Armed Forces.

As the helicopter crashed, she suffered two broken
arms, a broken finger, and a gunshot wound to her shoulder. In excruciating pain, her first thought upon regaining
consciousness was *Nobody's ever died from pain.*

She and another survivor were taken into captivity, and Major Cornum was held as a P.O.W. for a week. During that time, she was sexually assaulted by one of her captors. In an interview with the *New York Times*, she was remarkably calm about the experience and talked about how she was even calm at the time. She said, "[Sexual assault] ranks as unpleasant; that's all it ranks . . . I asked myself, 'Is it going to prevent me from getting out of here? Is there a risk of death attached to it? Is it permanently disabling? Is it permanently disfiguring? Lastly, is it excruciating?' If it doesn't fit one of those five categories, then it isn't important."

Major Cornum *decided* not to let her captors to have that impact on her. She took a step back from her experience even while it was occurring and reacted in a way that allowed her to have her preferred outcome—a quick release.

When she got home, she went back to work and rose to the rank of brigadier general, serving as an example for her daughter and everyone in the military.

Major Cornum is an extreme example of what is possible, and most people who have suffered sexual assault are not able to just decide not to let it affect them. She is an exception. But we can learn from her and use the power of deciding in our own lives, starting with smaller choices, and begin building that muscle, recognizing the tremendous potential of our own minds.

SILENT PRAYERS

When I was around 11 years old, I went running alone in the dark. I was staying in a cabin in Banff National Park with my aunts and uncles and grandparents. Everyone was watching television or had gone to bed, but I wanted to run and calm my mind. I didn't tell anyone where I was going—I slipped out the door and started running. I ran on a trail in the fading light beneath the twinkling stars in a state of bliss.

After running for a couple miles, I noticed someone behind me riding their bike on the trail in the dark. My intuition kicked in, my adrenaline started pumping, and I *knew* this person did not have the best of intentions. I tested my intuition by running off-trail through the trees. If he was just out for a bike ride, he would stay on the trail. If he went off the trail after me, he was out for something else.

He followed me, and as I sped up, so did he. It was clear to my 11-year-old mind that he was on a bicycle and I was on my two legs. He could catch me. Fear surged through my cells, my blood. No one knew where I was. There was no one else around.

All I could do was draw upon something I was taught as a little girl: the power of prayer and the understanding that I was a part of something bigger and that we are always surrounded by unseen forces, aiding us in our lives. I said a prayer in my mind, and I felt a sense of inner peace, a knowing that I would be divinely guided and protected. And then I became a witness to the power of remaining steadfast and full of faith and belief. My legs started to speed up. I darted in and out of those trees, making tight, unpredictable turns, running faster and farther than I ever had in my life.

After about a mile, I lost him. I made my way back to the cabin unhurt and unharmed, knowing that my speed

and agility, along with my calm mind in that moment, had
come from the power of asking through prayer and trusting and believing in this higher power.

ABUNDANCE ACTION

Chaos can look like a lot of different things—a predator,
a death in the family, extreme sickness, or losing a job. It
can look like tornadoes or mass destruction in a community, or the power going out. The timing of chaos can't be
predicted. It's simply not possible to be chaos-proof, but
we can be chaos-ready. Following these five steps can help
you get through chaos in just about any situation, whether
at home or at work, with a lot less stress and destruction,
and a lot more ease. Consider these action steps as a plan,
a way to manage your chaos effectively, whenever it arises.

1. **Prepare.** Preparation doesn't necessarily
   mean having all the necessary resources on
   hand, or having financial security, or mapping
   out all possible scenarios. Preparation starts in
   your mind as you prepare your inner being,
   your center, for whatever storms may come.
   Nothing is more vital than a daily breathing-
   and-centering practice mixed with intentional
   prayer. It allows you to anchor yourself and
   become steady when the wind blows. Take a
   deep breath for the count of seven, breathing
   as deeply as you can, past your chest, down

into your belly. Then slowly exhale for a count of seven. Repeat five times. Follow with an empowering intention and statement such as "I am divinely protected. Life is working for me."

2. **Devise a plan.** Try out the art of planning. For example, set aside time for a quick 5- to 10-minute gathering with your family each weeknight to talk about the upcoming day. What can you each do to support one another and avoid unnecessary chaos? The night before, write out the top five actions that you personally desire to take place, and see if you can get every member of your family to write their actions too. Write out one potential scenario that could come up that could steer you off your path, and strategize how you will handle the situation if it arises.

3. **Ask yourself,** *Who am I when chaos hits?* Visualizing who you want to be during times of chaos tends to drive the actions you will take when you are put in a situation of unpredictability. In situations of chaos, most people tend to place blame or panic, neither of which are helpful. How can you prepare to respond differently? How can you lean into infinite potentiality?

4. **Adjust.** Of course, you can't foresee everything. No matter how much you plan and

prepare, chaos will come sometimes despite all your efforts. When that happens, let go of your expectations, pivot, and move in a new way. Adjust your actions, your thinking, and your game plan. This becomes easier with practice, but all your preparation, especially your breath work, will support you, making you more likely to tune in to faith versus fear.

5. **Have a faithful attitude.** Attitude is everything in a time of chaos. The situation is the situation, and panicking, getting upset, or feeling defeated is not going to change it—in fact, it's likely to make it worse. When you remain calm and maintain hope and faith, you behave differently, and oftentimes produce a better outcome, not to mention a better experience for everyone involved. Peace breeds peace. Calm breeds calm. Faith breeds faith. Ask yourself, *What is the gift and lesson in this chaos? Why is this happening* for *me?*

CALMING CHAOS

While we can never control the chaos of life,
we can plan for it. To help you be prepared, I created a
simple print-on-demand chaos planner. Print it out,
go through the steps (with your family, ideally), and know
that whatever comes your way, you'll be ready!

www.EmbraceAbundanceBook.com/resources

HEALTH

*noun. the state of being free
from illness or injury; a person's mental
or physical condition*

be your
own hero

She remembered who she was and the game changed.

— Lalah Delia

Lesley's childhood home was abusive. For as long as she could remember, she was beaten daily and kept hungry. As the oldest, she tried to keep the peace and make sure her two younger brothers had enough to eat. This was her existence until age 15, when she left home to live on her own.

Unfortunately, things only got worse. Her best friend since kindergarten died in their freshman year of high school. In her sophomore year, her boyfriend died by suicide. In her junior year, another friend overdosed. It was death after death, and she had no one to turn to for help with her grief.

The weekend after her high school graduation, she and her boyfriend got married because he told her he would kill himself if she didn't marry him. A month later she was pregnant. She was 17 years old.

They remained married for 25 years, and he was abusive for most of them. She became pregnant a total of 19 times and bore 12 children. He insisted that she give birth at home, without assistance. She was her own midwife.

It was her children who saved her. They gave her the courage and power to save them and herself.

Despite all those years of abuse, Lesley knew deep down that there was more to life and that she owed it to her children to get them out of this situation and show them what happiness and safety could feel like. She fled, taking her children with her, and hid in the mountains of California until eventually she was able to secure a restraining order against her ex-husband and full custody of her children.

Lesley thought that she had finally escaped, but she soon realized that while she may have been free physically, she was still a prisoner in her mind. She couldn't ever be truly free until she began to heal her deep internal wounds. The pain and suffering that she endured for so many years left her so disconnected from herself, and she was merely trying to survive.

The years of trauma, starting from such an early age, had left her with PTSD and depression. Her self-esteem was low and her self-image was even lower. She had been yo-yo dieting for years—binging for comfort, and then starving to seek a sense of control. This cycle damaged her metabolism, and she suffered memory and muscle-tone loss.

Lesley felt like a molehill in a sea of mountains.

On her 50th birthday, she decided to try to see what it would be like to *not* feel lack, unworthiness, or that she was less than. She had tried many health programs before, but something about my 30-day challenge spoke to her. She signed up, trusting and hoping that somehow this would be different.

Within just a couple weeks of doing the challenge, Lesley felt so much hope! She experienced joy. Through healing foods, movement, and, most importantly, doing mindset meditation work, she began to learn how to love herself again and accept that she is *enough*. Her past did not define her future, and her pain became her fuel.

Through honoring herself through movement, Lesley made the decision to become her own hero. She has continued over the years to make movement, healing foods, and healing words parts of her daily routine, and she has released years of pain and trauma and emerged into a steady, loving, powerful woman.

Today she is creating a business, writing a book, and supporting other women, offering them tools to make positive changes in their own lives.

AROUND THE BLOCK

After I lost my son, Hap, I entered a deep depression. I remember so vividly moving from the bed to the couch to the bathroom. Sometimes to the kitchen, but only when the demands of hunger were overwhelming. As a trainer, I knew how important it was for me to move my body to get out of depression. But here's the thing about depression: it doesn't have motivation behind it.

Depression does have wisdom. It does have teaching. But you have to be the creator of momentum to receive that teaching. The runner's spirit in me was gone. I kept trying to muster the will to tie up my laces and go for a walk around the block. It seems simple, but somehow it became the hardest task imaginable. I wanted to stay in bed. My heart hurt, and I felt so much guilt and so much anger around the passing of my son.

But one day I managed to lace up my shoes and make that journey, shuffling around the block. I learned the power of movement on an even deeper level. With each step, my heart cracked open and the tears began to fall. The emotions that I'd been shoving down had only one place to go, and that was out.

Since that day, I have used movement as a profound way to heal and receive divine wisdom. I have seen thousands of clients around the world heal through movement, releasing layers of shame, guilt, and anger through each breath, each push, each drop of sweat—and use them as ways to tap into their inner wisdom.

Even today, as I write this book, I head out to nature to learn what the trees and rocks have to tell me. As I walk, my mind and heart expand as I make audio recordings of what wants to be expressed. And what I am called to tell you is this: move your body. As you move your body out in nature, whether it's through walking, speed walking, jogging, or running, you will heal the parts of you that want to be healed. You'll receive inner wisdom about your next best move, what you should say, what you should do, and how to honor yourself to the fullest.

Abundance is attracted to self-love and self-worth. When you say yes to *you* in full acceptance and love, miracles will start pouring in.

 ## ABUNDANCE ACTION

We know that the body and mind are intimately connected. The brain instructs the body to do certain things, but the body also instructs the brain. If we move our bodies with intention, we alter the chemical makeup of our cells and release feel-good chemicals which can alter how we think and feel. Movement can treat depression and anxiety, lifting the fog of these painful states so that we can find the will to unlayer more self-love and access our inner power. Music also has a way of moving us from our 3-D world into 4- and 5-D frequencies. These frequencies are reminders of our internal birthright to feel good and of our infinite power.

Get into your power through movement and music that lights you up. If you have a favorite way to move, plan to do it today. If you can, go for a walk, building up some perspiration. Run, jog, dance, or, if you are like me after having a baby or surgery, *shuffle*. Movement can help spur more motivation, deflate anxiety, lift your confidence, and remove brain fog. Aim for a realistic goal, whether that's 15 minutes or one mile.

MAGIC OF MOVEMENT

In our modern world, it's so easy to get out of practice with moving our bodies. To make things simple, you can find a beautiful, empowering, and most importantly *fun* 10-minute workout here:

www.EmbraceAbundanceBook.com/resources

power of love

❧

There is peace on earth
for him who sends good-will to man!

— FLORENCE SCOVEL SHINN

There once was a man who had been suffering for years, struggling with a terrible skin disease. He was a stage performer and was constantly trying to hide his dark, all-consuming rash from the audience. He had tried everything his doctors prescribed, and when that didn't work, he tried homeopathic measures, eating healing foods and cleaning his gut microbiome. His doctors told him it was incurable, and he fell into a state of despair.

One particular night he had an important stage performance. If he did well, it would set him up with other engagements. He was counting on this performance, for money had grown scarce. Opening night was a smashing success. The house was packed, and the critics raved. The man was elated.

The next day he received a notice of dismissal. Another member of the cast had been jealous of his success and had cunningly caused him to be released from the cast and future shows. The man was enraged. But instead of groveling in the rage, he knew he must turn it into love. That night he offered a prayer to God, asking for help in releasing his deep hate and anger.

He sat in silence for hours that night, working to send love and light to the person who had caused him so much pain. After some time a peace came over him, and a deep love for himself, the person who had hurt him, the director who had fired him, the rest of the cast—and the whole world. He continued sending love and feeling deep peace for all humanity for a total of three days and nights.

When he awoke on the fourth day, a miracle had happened. His skin disorder had disappeared. He had learned firsthand the power of love and forgiveness in complete healing.

JUNGLE WISDOM

I had been leading retreats, teaching and helping thousands of women, and operating a successful online health business for years, and as a leader and ever-learning student, I wanted to learn as many different modalities for healing as I possibly could. This led me on a seven-day deep immersion with a traditional healer, past the lush Costa Rican mountain jungles on a remote island. As we drove for hours and hours outside of San José, I began to get worried. This was either going to be the most amazing experience of my life . . . or I was going to get murdered.

Fortunately, once we got there, I settled into the idea that I was safe. It was peaceful and entirely murder-free. I spent the first day learning a lot and taking copious notes about ancient forms of healing within the body. But then the healer suddenly turned to me and said, "We need to work on your self-love."

Did we? I had spent years working on self-healing and self-worth. I had plenty of self-love, and this was not what I had come here for. He explained that if I was going to be a teacher, a healer in my own right, then I needed to go even deeper and do the work. I needed to uncover the hidden layers standing between me, my worth, and self-love.

As my days in the jungle wore on, my skin went haywire. White, pus-filled, inflamed pimples broke out all over my chin, neck, and mouth. I was eating well, consuming only natural, healing foods, and even in my most hormonal teenage years, I'd never experienced anything like this.

I knew I was deep in the jungle and there was no one to impress, but *I* was extremely self-conscious and uncomfortable with the pus that was forming on my face. I dug into my makeup bag and began rubbing tinted moisturizer on my face, trying to cover up what I could. And when the healer saw me hiding near the bathroom, looking at my face in a tiny mirror—the only one on the property—he said, so lovingly, "Why are you covering up your face?"

I said, "I'm putting on sunscreen."

He knew better. "Don't cover your skin. It's beautiful."

The healer walked over to a tree that happened to be placed perfectly next to the bathroom and handed me a piece of guanabana fruit. It had bumps and blemishes all over it. "This fruit is filled with healing properties. It is one of the most potent foods you can take for the ultimate healing of your organs," he said. "Like your skin, it has blemishes, but it accepts them and shows up in its healing power anyway. You need to do the same. Your body is talking to you. It is reminding you how through your thoughts, forgiveness, and claiming your worth, you can become your greatest healer. It is telling you that you have so many things you need to deliver to the world, things that are *inside* of you. You must show up in your power and be fully seen, even with your blemishes. Don't run from them. Don't try to hide them or cover them up. These blemishes are part of your growth and part of your power."

As I dove into my worthiness and looked at where I was holding on to resentment, anger, and guilt, my face cleared up, but so did other ailments in my body. The unknown cause of my neck pain went away when I forgave my ex, and my face became clear and radiant as I released internal mom guilt.

Over the years, I have had the privilege of coaching clients on the healing power of love and showing them that buried feelings do not die. Disease and unknown disorders can be caused by jealousy, hatred, unforgiveness, and fear.

The Bible says, "But I say to you, love your enemies, bless those who curse you, do good to those that hate you, and pray for those who spitefully use you, and persecute you" (Matthew 5:44). As you bring awareness to these emotions and send forgiveness, love, empowerment, and faith in its place, you generate a great aura of protection around you.

ABUNDANCE ACTION

Our bodies hold intelligence. They can tell us what emotion or past trauma we are carrying that wants to be released. They communicate with us through chronic pain, skin disorders, aches, disease, and misalignment in the body. When we discover how our mind, beliefs, and emotions affect our health, we can free ourselves from the mistruths we have been taught.

Here is a list of common chronic pain issues, along with the deep emotions and feelings that may be tied to these issues, asking to be expressed and released. Do any of these connections resonate for you?

Arthritis	—long-term tension or anger in life —depression endured over long periods of time —periods of anxiety or repressed anger —rigidity in your thinking
Bacterial colds	—unkind feelings toward someone —confusion in the home —belief in seasonal sickness

Flu virus	—general, unspecified fear or anxiety —belief in the likelihood of the worst possible outcomes —feelings of everything being out of your control
Lower back pain	—lack of financial support or feeling fear where money is concerned —desire to back out of something or wanting to run away from a situation —unexpressed anger
Fatigue	—burnout from a job or relationship —resistance to life —boredom
Headaches	—hurt feelings that you haven't expressed —exertion of too much pressure on yourself —belief that you haven't done enough

Insomnia	—tensions in life
	—deep-seated guilt
	—feelings of fear and anxiety
	—worry about your ability to do what is necessary
Neck Pain	—feelings of being under pressure
	—unexpressed feelings
	—inflexible state of mind
Overweight	—desire to protect your body
	—feelings of insecurity
	—feelings of self-rejection
Stomach problems	—threatened sense of security
	—fear of new ideas
	—lack of affection

Once you identify what you're experiencing, you can start to reframe your story and reshape the feeling that resonates or feels somewhat true for you through daily affirmations. Choose the opposite emotion, the emotion you want to experience, and speak it out loud with the words *I am*. For instance, "I am loved." Doing this every day for an extended period of time—at least several weeks—can release many of the ailments you may be experiencing in your body.

For example, if you are experiencing a headache, look at the emotion or feeling that could be tied to this sign felt in your body. Then state out loud the opposing, positive emotion:

> "I choose to communicate how I feel. I am communicating how I feel."

> "I choose to feel peace and I trust the process of life. I am releasing control."

Repeat these affirmations a few times each day for several weeks, taking deep, relaxing breaths as you send yourself and anyone who may be triggering these emotions deep love, white light, and understanding. Watch as you become your most powerful healer from the inside out.

power of food

❧

Tell me what you eat,
and I shall tell you what you are.

— Jean Anthelme Brillat-Savarin

After years spent drifting through her days with low energy, massive brain fog, and a consistently "blah" mood, Ashley was willing to try anything to feel better. She would feel exhausted by midafternoon but still wasn't able to fall asleep at night. When she would try to concentrate on projects at work, she couldn't focus, her mind wandering and unable to retain basic facts and figures. Worse even than the feelings in her body was the sense that her life just wasn't working out the way she wanted it to. She had taken a job "just for now," but that was 15 years ago. Her lack of direction wasn't getting her where she wanted to go. She knew she wanted to do something else, but she simply didn't have the willpower to do it. It was time for a change.

Ashley started eating whole, from-the-earth foods and stopped eating processed, chemical-laden foods and white sugars. Within days she felt her brain fog start to lift and her energy increase. This was so encouraging that she kept at it, adding meditation, time spent out in nature, and daily movement into the mix. With these simple changes, Ashley felt a deep connection to a higher power and noticed how, seemingly out of nowhere, the things she desired started showing up in her reality. From front-row parking spots to an out-of-the-blue message from the perfect networking contact, she was drawing into her life the exact things she desired. She left her "just for now" job, and with the help of her networking contact, she landed the job of her dreams.

BRAIN FOG

My head was pounding and my energy was faint as I shuffled my way to the kitchen to find something I could feed my four-year-old. She, on the other hand, was full of energy, smiling and chatting away, while I felt heavy with my brain full of fog. It had been a couple months since I had lost my son, and I couldn't shake the stuffiness in my brain and the depression that gripped my life.

Looking in the cupboard, I grabbed the quickest thing I could find—dry cereal. I knew that this wasn't the best thing to be feeding myself, let alone my beautiful, healthy four-year-old. I knew how to help myself with healthier food to ease depression, aches, pains, and brain fog. So why wasn't I doing it?

As I watched her spoon up her flaky cereal—my daughter with her cute blonde curls, red cheeks, and perfectly plump thighs—I made a pact to do right by her. Not just with what I gave her to consume but with what *I* was consuming, so I could be a better mother. That day I started researching foods that had positive effects on the brain and the nervous system, particularly depression. I bought superfood ingredients with potent medicinal powers and experimented with recipes in my small kitchen. I fed these foods to myself and my daughter, and within the first week of eating these superfoods, I felt clearer. Getting up in the morning became easier. I felt a heavy weight begin to slide off my shoulders. My daughter was calmer and better able to handle all the small challenges that come with childhood. And after two weeks, I was feeling motivation.

After months of being stuck in a deep depression, I was amazed to feel a sense of wanting to get up and get out, to *do* something. I was witnessing firsthand the power of food in feeding the soul. Feeling more positive, more energized, and clearer made it easier for me to move into action toward what I was desiring, *and* I also was becoming more of a magnet for situations, people, and scenarios that supported my dreams.

Those days of playing with healing superfoods in my kitchen led to my creation of healing food programs for millions of people around the globe. I had witnessed how good, whole foods could heal the body not only on a physical level but also mentally and spiritually. And I have watched as my clients felt better in their bodies, increasing their feel-good energy and sending that frequency out into the world.

Everything is made of energy. Food, thoughts, and actions all hold a frequency—"dead" food has a low vibration, while living, nutrient-dense food has a high vibration.

Your job is to match the frequency of what you desire to the frequency you hold internally. Food, movement, and thought can all change the energy in your body to match the frequency of what you desire. It's like a radio that you need to tune. For example, if you want to listen to 74.5 FM, but you tune only to 74.4, you'll get static and some music. Tune to 74.6 and you'll also get static and some music. It's only if you tune to exactly 74.5 that your music will come in perfectly clearly. Your goal is to tune your energy to match the frequency of what you want. Once you do, your music will come in loud and clear, serving as a magnet to bring your desires into being.

When we're eating foods with the right nutritional components, our cells are better able to run at an optimum. This peak cellular function raises our energy and therefore our energetic vibration, which then attracts to us things that vibrate at the same high level. When we operate at a higher vibration, the manifesting floodgates open, and we become magnets for what we desire. When you choose healing foods, you affirm to the Universe and God that you feel you are worthy of the best. When you feel good, you do good.

ABUNDANCE ACTION

For the next two weeks, eat *only* high-vibration, healing foods that come directly from the earth. If you have to wash the dirt away, welcome it into your body! If you have to open a package or read through a long list of ingredients, leave it on the shelf. Within the first week, your energy levels will begin to go up, and by the second week, the experiences in your life will begin to match the experience of being in your body.

When you're choosing what food to eat, think about whether it's artificial or comes from nature. If you want to increase your vibration and overall health, you'll want to avoid artificial foods whenever possible. How do you figure that out? Well, let's take a look at the layout of the grocery store. You'll find most natural foods on the perimeter of the store, whether they are fresh fruits and vegetables, herbs, meats, eggs, grain, or dairy. In the middle aisles, you'll find foods that are manufactured or highly processed, like crackers, chips, prepackaged breads and desserts, sodas, candies, and even packaged meals. These foods are loaded with toxins and preservatives so they have a longer shelf-life, making them more chemical than food. They increase body fat, surround your organs with toxins, cause brain fog and irritability, and contribute to a whole host of health problems.

I've provided a link to a meal plan that goes into more detail, but here are some overall guidelines:

- **Fruits and vegetables.** Eat six servings per day.

- **Protein.** Eat some form of protein in every meal, whether it comes from meat or not. If you're avoiding meat, you can choose Greek yogurt, eggs, kefir, chickpeas or other legumes, or raw nuts and seeds. Even certain vegetables like kale contain some protein.

- **Grains and complex carbohydrates.** Add these in slowly, up to three servings a day, and choose wisely. Sweet potatoes, brown rice, and quinoa are all good options—and quinoa has some protein!

- **Healthy fats.** Fresh avocado, raw unsalted nuts and seeds, coconut oil, and olive oil are all good options, but you'll want to avoid processed oils like canola and vegetable oil. Eat up to three to four tablespoons a day.

- **Water.** Remember, your body is 70 percent water! Flush it out often by drinking up to one gallon a day of water.

YOUR BODY IS A TEMPLE

We show our reverence for our beautiful bodies with the foods we eat. I've compiled some of my best healthy recipes into an abundance meal plan that you can download—totally free—here:

www.EmbraceAbundanceBook.com/resources

counting sheep

♥

A good laugh and a long sleep
are the two best cures for anything.

— Unknown

Irene had tried everything.

Whenever she mentioned her insomnia, the person she was talking to, whether they were a friend, a relative, or just a random acquaintance, would ask, "Oh, have you tried ____?" Every single person had an idea for her. "Have you tried melatonin?" "Have you tried meditation? "Have you tried jogging? Exercise makes you tired!"

And every single time, Irene would smile and say, "Yes, thanks, I tried that, and it just didn't work." She could fall asleep, but she just couldn't stay that way.

As she continued to work to find rest, Irene discovered what was keeping her awake: she was. When Irene would wake up in the middle of the night, she would try to turn off her mind. She would look away from her worries and grab a book and try to distract herself back to sleep. And when those worries were about something small that didn't really matter in the long run, she would eventually get back to sleep.

But then there would be nights when she would lie awake and sleep simply would not come. And on those nights, the worries would not be simple, and they would not be coming from her mind. They were whisperings from her heart.

When Irene finally began to listen, and when she was brave enough to start removing people and situations from her life that were keeping her up at night, she was at last able to sleep deeply and through the night.

NOISE

I was in a region of the Yucatán that was sparsely populated and rich in Mayan culture. The other members of the circle were healers and tribe members who lived in the area. We were enjoying each other's company, laughing and sipping cacao by the evening fire. As the night went on and the stars were bright in the sky, the leader of the circle spoke up. We grew quiet and listened intently as he explained that when we can't sleep, it's because the souls of our ancestors are trying to speak to us. They are trying to get our attention, usually between 3 and 5 A.M.

As humans, we have tuned out our inner peace, our quiet, our whisperings, and our wisdom by becoming so preoccupied with the busyness of life—phones, TV, the next Netflix hit, and the news—that our souls cannot be heard above the noise. Our circle leader told us that our soul is trying to communicate at night, when we are off our phone, off the news, and still. And we silly humans are now busy trying to figure out ways to remove the soul talk at night too. We look at our soul talk as a disruption, and we feel like we can't get any good sleep.

This conversation hit me so hard, because I'm in the world of health, and everyone is always talking about ways to biohack our way into deeper, restful sleep. They suggest different tonics and pills, all while stretching and turning off your phone at night, making sure your room stays dark and comforting yourself with a weighted blanket. These can all help you find a deeper, more profound sleep, but it's possible you may be missing the most important sleep ingredient of all—listening to your internal guidance system, the whisperings of your soul.

We have forgotten to slow down, be in nature, do what we love, and be with whom we love. If you wake in the night, your soul may be trying to get your attention when your mind is quiet enough for it to be heard. Perhaps it is sharing with you that you are in a job that isn't fulfilling your truest expression. Perhaps it is trying to tell you that you are in a relationship that is keeping you from living out your passion and purpose, or eating foods or hanging out with people that are keeping you from your deepest happiness.

Ever since that night in the Yucatán, when I wake up in the wee hours, I no longer look at it as an inconvenience. Instead I ask, "What would you have me know?" Oftentimes my soul is simply asking me to think about what's true for me. Other times it's asking me to get up, write, commune with my higher self, and ask, *What is it I truly choose in life? What is in the highest service of me and humanity? Where can I tweak my life to become more aligned with my soul's purpose? What can I turn off and tune in to to be honoring more of me?*

ABUNDANCE ACTION

Deep sleep allows our bodies to recover and heal. It is also the gateway to aligning with abundance. The following are some suggestions for ways to create profound healing through sleep.

1. Plan for seven to nine hours of sleep. That means going to bed early enough to allow yourself time to fall asleep and *still* get those seven to nine hours before you have to get up in the morning.

2. Thirty minutes to an hour before going to bed, turn off all your electronic devices, including the TV and the phone. They disrupt your nervous system and make it hard to fall asleep.

3. Try taking a hot bath with Epsom salts and lavender essential oil to cleanse the day away, and a destressing stretch or a deep-sleep meditation, or both.

4. Have a cup of decaf tea before bed! You can try chamomile tea, Sleepytime tea, or valerian

tea if you want a gentle sedative thrown in there. I like to add raw honey to my tea. Honey is known to help some people fall into deeper sleep.

5. Block out excess light and add just a touch of weight to your eyes, particularly if you are more sensitive to light than others. Covering your eyes with something soft can help you relax more deeply.

6. Consider a weighted blanket, particularly if you struggle with anxiety. The weight creates a feeling of grounding within the nervous system and mimics a giant snuggle or hug.

7. Turn off the noise of the day. Turn off social media and the news. Tune in to yourself through gratitude, journaling, meditation, and time spent in nature.

8. Take some time, maybe 5 or 10 minutes, to listen to your inner being, center, spirit, or soul. If you are not taking time to listen during the hustle and bustle of your life, your spirit may try to nudge you at night when you are not distracted. Ask yourself, *Am I living the life that is for my highest good? Am I surrounding myself with people who help me be the highest version of myself? Am I operating from a place of love or fear?*

dance on tables

❧

Play is the highest form of research.

— ALBERT EINSTEIN

On a calm December evening on Necker Island, Richard Branson received a tweet from an American woman, Shannon Smith, saying she'd like to spend a day in his shoes. So the Branson-esque move was, of course, to literally send her his shoes. "Without hesitation, I took my shoes off, walked over to the office and set about sending her my size elevens," he wrote. He challenged Smith to wear them for a full day or else give them back. Smith answered the challenge and shuffled around in his too-large shoes all day on Christmas Eve while she volunteered at a homeless shelter.

As the founder of Virgin Atlantic and several other companies, Branson is massively successful in business—and he has a lot of fun doing it. I have a close friend who once shared a story with me of a time he and his wife went to visit Branson on Necker Island. He had made the trip with the intention of capturing some wisdom.

They gathered around the table under the stars, eating and drinking, and my friend asked Branson for the key to his success.

At first it seemed like Branson was ignoring the serious question. He looked past my friend to his wife and said, "Your wife is beautiful. Do you see how beautiful she is?" Then Branson literally climbed up on the table where they were all eating, pulled my friend's wife up with him, and they started dancing. Branson looked down at my friend, laughing, and said, "Being in the moment and having fun. That is the key to success."

Branson not only lives this way; he also cultivates it within his company. Virgin is a safe space for joy and fun. And not the kind of corporate "fun" we all dread—icebreakers and forced camaraderie and cheer—but genuine joy and love, which makes the employees happier and more creative. As Branson says, "The fact that I have a lot of fun doing what I'm doing means that the 60–70,000 people that work for Virgin enjoy what they're doing, and they're proud of what they're doing and they know they can do it with a smile."

COUCHES

For the longest time, I had no clue what it meant to have fun or be childlike. I grew up on a farm in a small town in Idaho. I knew work. I knew getting up early because weeds needed pulling, gardens needed planting, floors needed scrubbing, and all the animals needed feeding. We trekked mountains in the winter to hunt our own meat, and then we cut it up and packaged it for the long winter season. I spent hours in the sun picking beans, snapping their ends and heads off and doing a final snap down the middle, to place them in a jar for the canning process.

My idea of fun was getting to come inside to snap the beans. I would lay out a big blanket on the floor, set the bucket in front of me, and watch a soap opera on our black-and-white TV while I snapped away. Fun was sprinkled in every now and again, but it always had a twinge of guilt to it. If you were having fun, something wasn't getting done. I stepped into adulthood with this story in my cells. If I wasn't busy, I wasn't worthy. If I wasn't busy, I wasn't enough. If I wasn't busy, I was lazy.

I fidget, especially on couches. They remind me of this underbelly current of unworthiness and laziness. My teenage daughter has seen me fidget her whole life, and she can see right through it. She's always been our unforgiving truth teller, a sage wrapped up in a 17-year-old body. Recently, she looked me dead in the eye and said, "You need to learn to relax. This would be your greatest work. Learning to relax and have some fun."

I was offended. "What do you mean? I am in a constant state of fun. I live my purpose and passion and have made it my life's work."

"When was the last time you did something fun that didn't make any sense or help someone else or fit in the role of your work?"

I sat there for a moment and didn't fidget. Then I got up and got busy.

Her truth rang in my cells for a few days and then I made it my mission to learn how to relax and have some fun.

When I started to make "having fun" a priority in my life, everything began to line up for me even faster, and my overall health increased. Craig and I have made it a weekly ritual to literally schedule fun into our lives. When we look at our calendar for the week, we add one fun item into each day's agenda—whether that's a bike ride, a hike, a lunch date, a conversation with an old friend, or simply watching a comedy. And if we're going on a business trip, we always schedule an extra day that we set aside for exploring, adventure, and romance.

As busy people, we often leave fun as the last ingredient in the recipe of our lives when it should be the first. Fun is how to live and create a healthier, more magnetic, and manifesting life. When we follow the good vibes, it is easier to feel the high vibrations in our cells, which then turn us into magnetic forces for more good in our lives.

There are so many proven health benefits to increasing the level of fun in your life. People who make having fun and enjoying life a priority are shown to have reduced stress, higher levels of serotonin, better sleep, higher energy levels, improved memory and concentration skills, and better relationships.

I am still working on relaxing and creating more fun in my life. I want my girls to know that doing more doesn't make them worth more just as much as I want them to understand the power of play to release stress and gain more creativity and self-love, so they can become powerful connectors to divine intelligence.

ABUNDANCE ACTION

It can be surprisingly difficult to create activities that we genuinely enjoy, especially if we have created routines and patterns that involve getting a high from crossing off our to-do list, mindlessly scrolling through social media, or watching TV at the end of the day. When was the last time you genuinely had *fun*? Hosting a barbecue is supposed to be fun, but it isn't if you are not the type who likes to host parties or cook and clean up. Watching a movie is supposed to be fun, but sometimes you feel like you need to watch the next Oscar contender when really all you want to do is laugh at the latest crass comedian. The key is to find activities that *you* enjoy as well as something that is intriguing and new.

When you are in a state of joy, you become a magnet for even more joy. You begin to attract the dreams in your heart through your play. So make time to do something fun today! Keep it simple, and keep it focused on *you*. For the next seven days, I want you to schedule a little bit of fun every day. Maybe your calendar can look something like this:

—**Monday:** Set a timer around lunchtime, and when it goes off, turn your speakers all the way up, play your favorite song, and *dance* for no good reason!

—**Tuesday:** Stop by YouTube and spend a few minutes doing some laughter yoga. (Yes, this is a real thing, and it's a blast!)

—**Wednesday:** If you have a pet, be ridiculously silly with them for five minutes until you're laughing so hard you're in tears. If you don't have one, stop by your local shelter and get some cuddles in!

—**Thursday:** Explore a part of your neighborhood you've never spent time in or walk a different path than you're used to.

—**Friday:** Sing! Even if you're terrible at it! Crank up something fun like "Bohemian Rhapsody" and belt it out.

—**Saturday/Sunday:** Go on an adventure, whatever that means to you! Maybe it's tubing or zip-lining or exploring in some nearby woods.

Whatever you choose to do, remember that this time isn't meant to do anything for you other than let you have a good time—and that's doing *plenty*.

RELATIONSHIPS

*noun. the way in which two or
more concepts, objects, or people are connected;
the state of being connected*

completion
conversations

❧

Most people don't listen with the intent to understand;
they listen with the intent to reply.

— STEPHEN COVEY

My friend Kate was all dressed up. She and her friend
Jen were going out for a long-planned girls' night, and she
couldn't wait. Jen had moved to the neighboring town,
and they hadn't seen each other in over six months. They
were going to go for drinks and then to a concert, because
their favorite band was playing. When Jen picked her up,
Kate kissed her husband good-bye, jumped into the car,
and greeted her friend. "You look *fantastic*! Wow, I've really been excited about this."

Jen nodded but didn't say anything.

Kate frowned. Normally Jen was the gushy one, and
Kate was the quiet one. And this whole night out had been
Jen's idea! "So, do you want to grab a drink first, or should

we go straight to the club? I found this amazing craft beer place—we could go there?"

Jen shrugged. "If you want."

Now, Kate didn't even like beer, but Jen did, and Kate had gone to all the trouble of choosing something she knew her friend would like. She felt a little hurt that Jen hadn't noticed. Kate took a deep breath, telling herself to let it go. "Hey, I'm so glad we're doing this. We haven't been able to spend as much time together lately, and I've really missed you."

Jen didn't say anything at all. It was like she hadn't even heard.

Kate's eyes pricked with tears. Jen obviously didn't feel the same way. Why were they even going out together? What was the point if they didn't have anything to talk about anymore? Kate felt abandoned, even though her friend was sitting right there. She tried one last time. "Jen," she said. "You're not really talking to me, and it feels like you don't want to be here. Are you angry with me, or is it that maybe, since you moved, we aren't such good friends anymore?"

To Kate's amazement, Jen started to cry. Jen pulled the car over and explained that she and her husband were having troubles, and seeing Kate kissing *her* husband good-bye had made Jen feel like a failure in her own marriage. She had been jealous and didn't know how to talk about that, especially since she and Kate hadn't had those kinds of close conversations in some time.

By sharing vulnerability, both were able to get to the truth of what was really going on, and to grow and heal. Kate was able to recognize how she had made up a story in her mind about their friendship based on Jen's reactions. Had they not communicated vulnerably, and had Kate gone along with the untrue story in her mind, most likely there would have been a fight or a falling-out between dear friends.

TOOTHPASTE

One busy morning Craig walked into the bathroom to brush his teeth, when he discovered that *his* very own toothpaste was lying out with crusties on the top. He started to get angry, and a story was beginning to take shape. "Danette doesn't respect my things. Heck, she doesn't respect my time. Now I have to clean this off and hope to get some toothpaste out so I can brush my teeth. She is so insensitive to leave it open like that. How long does it really take to put the cap back on and put it in the drawer? Why doesn't she just buy her own toothpaste? She is so irresponsible!"

His stories were escalating quickly, and because he knew this was not going to be good for our relationship or having snuggle time with me later, he approached me and said, "Can we have a completion conversation about something later today? Let me know a time and place that works for you."

We settled on later in the evening, when the kids were done eating and doing their homework. We went out for a walk so we could have some privacy, and Craig presented me with the facts of what happened: I used his toothpaste. And then he calmly laid out how it made him feel: like I don't respect his things, his space, or his feelings.

My only job in that moment was to listen. To truly listen. Not to justify or validate or explain. I then put myself in his shoes. I thought of an instance when I felt like this before.

I thought about when my daughter borrowed my sweater and returned it dirty, and how that made me feel like she didn't consider my things or me when she borrowed my stuff and didn't take care of it. I told him, "I can see how it would feel like I'm not thinking about you. I'm sorry."

And Craig said, "Thank you. I appreciate that you get it."

How I chose to respond next is key to completion conversations. I told him the things I would do to make sure it wouldn't happen again—either using my own damn toothpaste or at least giving him the consideration to close it properly. "Are we complete?"

"Yes," Craig said. "We're complete."

Seems pretty simple, right? And yet our conversations with our partners, our children, our friends, and our co-workers hardly ever go this smoothly. There are a couple reasons why this works, and while they seem insignificant, they matter enormously.

The first step is asking to have the conversation *later*. This is so important, because if you try to have this discussion while you're triggered, it's going to go very poorly. If the issue matters enough to you to have a conversation about it, then it's important enough for you to wait until you're calm enough to discuss it rather than yelling or fighting about it.

It's also helpful to give your spouse a little bit of a heads-up. I know that when Craig comes to me with a request for a completion conversation, I often think, *Oh crap, what did I do now?* That warning allows me to give the situation some thought, and most of the time I know what he's going to say and what my role was in the situation before we even talk.

And, often enough, I'll have something I want to bring up too. The important thing to do when that happens is to *complete* the completion conversation before turning to another topic. Keep it clean. Otherwise it devolves into "Well, *you* did . . ." and we all know how that turns out. Remember this is someone you care about, and you want to make sure they feel it! You've done something that hurt them—and that happens. What matters most is acknowledging it and moving forward with love and peace.

Think about it this way: Do you want to be right, or do you want to be happy?

The next point is the apology. Say back to the person how it would make you feel if you were in their shoes, and then apologize without being defensive. If I'd said, "I was in a rush," or "I did that because you forgot to buy my toothpaste," I'd have been offering an excuse that would have made Craig feel like I didn't validate his feelings and understand the impact I'd had.

Again, do you want to be right, or do you want to be happy?

Craig had to play a part in this too. He had to forgive me after my apology. Once you believe that someone knows their impact and has laid out steps they will take to make sure it doesn't happen again, you need to let it go and genuinely forgive them. Remember, you love them and want them to be happy too. Holding a grudge helps no one.

Those you love deserve your vulnerability. They deserve you unraveling deep, untruthful stories you slowly but surely could start putting between one another. The success of anything you do in life can be measured by the number of tough conversations you're willing to have.

ABUNDANCE ACTION

The completion conversation is an extremely effective tool for any relationship—with your best friend, your children, your family members, or your employees. When we clear the energy of frustration or hurt, our frequency becomes more attuned to love and acceptance, which creates a smoother, more magnetic path to more abundance.

For your next difficult conversation, give this a try:

Step One. Ask. "Can we have a completion conversation today?" Set a time and place.

Step Two. Calmly present your partner with what happened and how it made you feel.

Step Three. Your partner says they can understand how that made you feel, perhaps by providing an example of how this may have happened to them, and then apologizes.

Step Four. If you still do not feel understood, your partner should try to explain how they understand in a different way.

Step Five. Once it's clear that they understand, forgive them. Ask, "In the future, how can we avoid this happening again?"

Step Six. Your partner offers suggestions for how they will avoid repetition, though you should be aware that mistakes will happen.

Step Seven. Your partner asks, "Are we complete?" and you respond, "Yes. We are complete."

If both parties want to have their own completion conversations, make sure those conversations are kept separate. The person who first approached with the request should go first, and only after that conversation has reached completion can the other person begin their topic.

COMPLETION CONVERSATIONS

Nothing will change your life faster than having authentic conversations with all of your relationships.
To help you through the process the first few times, I put together a completion checklist at
www.EmbraceAbundanceBook.com/resources

when not to fix it

*Just when the caterpillar thought
the world was over, it became a butterfly.*

— CHUANG TZU

A little boy was playing outdoors when he found a fascinating caterpillar. He carefully picked it up and took it home to show his mother. He asked her if he could keep it, and she said he could if he took good care of it.

The little boy got a large jar. He filled it with plants to eat and sticks to climb on. Every day he watched the caterpillar.

One day the caterpillar climbed up a stick and started acting strangely, and the boy got worried. His mother explained that the caterpillar was creating a cocoon and would soon change into a butterfly. The little boy was thrilled to hear about the changes his caterpillar would go through. He watched every day, waiting for the butterfly to emerge. Finally, it happened—a small hole appeared in the cocoon. The little boy watched the butterfly struggle to come out.

He got worried again. The butterfly was having such a hard time, and the little boy didn't want it to suffer. He ran to get scissors, and then walked back (he had learned not to run with scissors), and carefully snipped the cocoon to make the hole bigger. The butterfly broke free with ease.

The butterfly didn't look quite right. It had a swollen body and small, shriveled wings. The boy watched the butterfly, waiting for the wings to dry out and expand, but it never happened.

The butterfly spent the rest of its life crawling around with its swollen body and shriveled wings.

It was never able to fly.

This bothered the little boy for years, and eventually he learned that this had happened because of *him*. Despite his best intentions, he had actually hurt the butterfly by helping it. The butterfly was *supposed* to struggle, as its efforts to make its way out of the cocoon would push the fluid out of its body and strengthen its wings. It needed to work and struggle in order to fly.

POPCORN

One afternoon I got a call from the elementary school. It was around 1 P.M., and my mind raced at what could possibly be wrong. It's the kind of call you dread, because it comes before 3 P.M., when school hasn't been released. I thought that they must be calling about Sarah, who was eight at the time. She must have been sick, or there was a fire, or she did something that required a parent conversation.

I answered reluctantly, "Hello."

The voice on the other end took a deep breath and said, "We have noticed that Sarah spends every day alone on the playground. She doesn't have any friends. We're worried about her, and we feel we need to do something about this. We thought we would give you a call."

My motherly instincts went into overdrive, and I wanted to fix any aches and pains my daughter must be feeling by not having any friends and feeling alone. I went into panic mode. I started making plans in my head—we would invite over all the girls I knew, and we would serve the best popcorn, have movies and games, and ensure she was the most popular girl in school. Instead, all I could say was, "Thanks for informing me. I will talk to her."

When Sarah came home later that evening, I sat her down and asked, "Why are you alone?" And her answer surprised me.

"Because the girls are kind of mean. One day they like you and the next they push you out. I don't know what day is going to be my day. I choose to have nice friends. Until they are nice friends, I would rather be by myself. I kind of like it."

That day I realized a powerful truth about what happens when we try to fix those we love. Sarah was guiding herself and trusting her own instincts. She was choosing love. She was standing in bravery as she chose herself and kindness. As parents we often feel it's our job to worry for our children or loved ones. But the greatest gift we can give anyone is our unwavering faith, putting their lives in the hands of God, trusting that they are divine beings and are divinely guided. When we allow this, we give them a great aura of protection.

 **ABUNDANCE ACTION**

Take a truthful inventory of how you approach your relationships. Are you trying to fix or remove pain from the people you love? Write down their names.

Now think of a time when you went through a challenging situation and you handled it on your own in your own way. How did that feel? What did it teach you? Did you build resilience, compassion, or a deeper kind of wisdom *because* of that struggle?

Today let the people you've been trying to fix know that you love them. Let them know you are sorry for trying to fix them and remove this amazing gift of growth that has been presented to them. Tell them you believe in their innate strength and resilience. That you know that what they are going through is going to make them stronger, more resilient, and more compassionate.

This will provide them with the knowledge that they are strong, capable, and can trust in the process of life and the fact that you believe in them.

free bird

You must love in such a way
that the person you love feels free.

— THICH NHAT HANH

Once upon a time, there was a lost baby bird. She was sweet and had fluffy little feathers and no one to take care of her. A woman found her in the woods and brought her home, where she fed and cared for her. They loved each other, and as the baby bird grew older, she developed two perfect, brightly colored wings, full of glossy feathers. She taught herself to fly, and every day she flew freely through the sky and brought joy to everyone who saw her.

As the woman watched the bird, her eyes shone with pride and with love. Every day the bird soared off, but every day she returned, and the woman adored her.

However, as time went by, the woman became afraid. What if the bird wanted to fly far away? What if this time she never came back? Then the woman would be alone. She thought, *I'm going to set a trap. The next time the bird comes home to me, I will make it so she will never leave me again.*

The bird returned the day after she left, like she always did, for she loved the woman. And so she never anticipated what came to pass: the woman put her in a cage.

The woman kept her there and admired her every day. She fed and watered her until one day, something strange happened. The woman found that the bird wasn't what she'd been. Her feathers started to lose their gloss and bright colors. And after a while, the woman paid her less attention and didn't fawn over her or care for her, and the bird began to waste away. Then one day she died.

The woman mourned what she had lost, but she didn't mourn the bird in the cage. What she remembered was the beautiful, spirited bird who had soared high in the clouds.

LEASHES

Yesterday I was running with my dog Ollie in the fields and paths near our home. Running is my happy place. It's where I meet my stories, observe them, and resolve them with each stride. It's where I get to run away for a moment and be okay with my sweat, my stinkiness, my unkempt hair, and my exhaustion and drown out the noise of the world with the loudness of my heartbeat.

Where I run, dogs are asked to be on leashes. I understand the concept. I really do, but the deep-down wild part of me hates it. I have felt like I have been on a leash my whole life.

Don't go where others are asked not to.

Don't ask too many questions.

Don't be too wild.

Stay on the straight and narrow.

Stay in line, walk where others are walking, and walk at their pace.

I get up early, when most people are sleeping, so that I can unclip Ollie's leash and watch her run, wild and unbridled in the open field. I live for that moment. I find my truth in her joy, in her freedom, in her speed. I watch as she feels the wind in her ears. Nothing makes me happier.

There have been many times when I have sat on a couch facing a friend, a C.E.O., or a celebrity. I have spent time in nature, walking side by side and hearing their truthful stories about the cages they have built around themselves. It turns out that most of these cages look like a big, beautiful home with the best coffee maker, a machine that grinds beans and spits out a perfect latte at the touch of a button. The cage looks like a whole closet full of shoes where, when you walk in, it feels like you're stepping into the shoe section at Nordstrom. The cage looks like a relationship that is built on an appearance of love and fun, but in the quiet of the night is made of two souls who feel miles apart. It's not that the big house, the coffee maker, or the shoes are making them unhappy—it's that they're not truly living their purposeful, vibrant, soulful existence.

I often ask people, "How would you spend your time if money didn't matter? If you were not worried about hurting those you love, what would you do? What would be true for you?"

A lot of times they will tell me, "I just want to live simply. I want to have passion. I want to feel desire in my relationship. I don't want to wear these suits anymore. I want to take my mornings nice and slow and soulfully. When I make love with my partner, I want to feel like we're connecting on a deeper level, that there's deep trust and unconditional love—and that this love is not contingent on how much money I make or how much success I seem to have."

From the outside, this sounds so simple. But the truth is that so many of us have leashed ourselves to a life we thought we wanted, a life that society said was right and good, and we forgot about the truth of what our soul wanted. Society has mapped out an existence that we believe will make us happy. So we clip on a leash that tethers us to what we think is right and safe. We keep ourselves in line, attached to society's expectations.

But here's the painful truth: There is no safe marriage or relationship. At any moment, disaster could hit, and all the illusory safety parameters you have put in place could come crumbling down. And in your attempt to remain safe, you may have traded away all those vibrant colors of feeling free.

Love, passion, and pain are the very essence of being. This interplay is the subject of every book, movie, song, or work of art. The dance between pleasure, pain, and uncertainty is what *living* is.

So what would happen if you unhooked that leash? What if you let the people you love be themselves in all their dimensions, even if it means they will fly away for a little while? What if you opened the cage you have put around yourself? What if you stopped doing the things you thought were "right" and did what made you feel alive?

What if you picked up that brush and painted because it felt good? What if you stripped off your clothes and danced naked and let your hips sway? What if you howled, cried, and spoke the deepest truths that made everyone uncomfortable . . . and allowed others the possibility to free their own truths too?

What if you made love simply to enjoy each stroke and caress, each sway, each movement just for the sake of it? Not to get anywhere, not to finish, not to orgasm or wonder if you are doing it right or saying the right things. What if you just let your body do what it knows? What if you allowed yourself this simple freedom and allowed your partner the same?

Where can you be a little more wild, a little more free, to run abandoned in wide-open spaces?

 ## ABUNDANCE ACTION

Where can you release yourself today? Can you take off the practical clothes that give you no thrill and put on what makes you feel alive, relaxed, or sexy? Can you say what you've always wanted to say?

Where can you release the cages you've built around those you love in the illusion of safety?

Today, tell your partner or children, or both, that you want to release them. Tell them what you saw in them when you met and what drew you in and made you love them. Ask how you can allow them to live a little bit more as the multicolored, vibrant being they are.

Listen. Don't talk. Step into what they share.

be the
energetic match

The law of attraction is this: You don't attract what you want. You attract what you are.

— DR. WAYNE DYER

Annie had never had a true romantic partnership, where each person loves, supports, and enjoys the other without losing themselves. She had moved in and out of relationships, and none of them filled her up or gave her what she thought she needed. She always felt like she was struggling to please, struggling to be seen, and struggling to be loved.

A part of her decided to write off relationships entirely. She told herself it was for the best, but deep down she still longed for what she saw others had—someone to share fun times with, to grow with, and to explore life with.

Another part of her knew there was a higher way. She sent love and complete forgiveness to her past loves and herself. With the extra time she had previously used to spend going out with dates or friends who didn't fulfill her, Annie began to work on *herself*. Rather than trying to make her external relationships be what she needed them to be, she started becoming and doing what she desired. She supported herself, giving herself encouragement when she felt uncertain. She had fun, went on adventures, laughed at herself, and did things she enjoyed. She filled herself up so much that she eventually became her own best friend. She felt complete.

She discovered that one of her favorite thing to do was to walk in the park. She lived in a city, and there wasn't much green space, and none of her past relationships had enjoyed going to the park, so she hadn't been in a while. She found a lovely little park close to her neighborhood, and she would go there as often as she could. She even discovered a favorite bench right under a lilac tree.

One unusually beautiful day, she headed over to her favorite bench, excited to sit and soak in the sun, but she discovered that this normally empty bench was now occupied. There was a man sitting there, good-looking but not as conventionally handsome as the men she'd been attracted to in the past. Ordinarily Annie would have walked away and found another bench to sit on. But this was her favorite bench, and surely there was room for two. When she asked if she could sit down, the man smiled at her and moved over to give her space. She explained that this was her favorite bench in her favorite park, and it turned out it was his favorite too. They marveled that they had never run into each other before this.

They had such a nice time talking that they decided to go for coffee. And they enjoyed the conversation over coffee so much that they made plans to go for a bike ride the next day. Their friendship developed over time and eventually it became the relationship that Annie had been longing for, filled with fun and passion.

These two souls had both worked internally to fill themselves up before meeting. They were each coming from a place of wholeness, allowing their partnership to be unlike anything they had experienced before. Once Annie realized that finding the right relationship started with her internal healing work, the rest was history.

CREATING SPACE

When Emma reached out to me for coaching, I thought she was coming for business advice to take her growing venture to the next level. After all, she had everything we tend to think of as desirable: she was beautiful and athletic and had the freedom and money to take lavish vacations and a business that was growing and doing well. But it turned out she wanted coaching about how to attract the right partner.

"I have this story," Emma explained to me. "I believe that no man I would want to be with wants to be with a successful, independent woman. I believe I'm unlovable because I'm successful. And I'm carrying so much sadness because I just don't seem to be able to find the loving, long-term partner I can adore and love."

And because of her story, the men she was meeting *were* threatened by her success, and she did not begin to form a vulnerable connection after the second date.

"I hear you," I said. "I can help you with this. The first thing I need to do is take a look at your home."

Emma's home was gorgeous. She had a two-car garage, a sprawling king-size bed, and a massive walk-in closet. But here's the thing—that beautiful, enormous closet was packed tight with Emma's clothes. There was no room for anyone else. I instructed Emma to clear out a section of her closet, leaving it empty and waiting. I told her to sleep on just one side of that spacious bed, and to park her car on one side of the garage, not in the middle.

By doing this, she was letting the Universe know that she had space in her life for the partner she wanted.

Secondly, I had her write out everything she desired to feel and experience in her partnership. Emma wrote a vision of a man who accepted her as powerful and independent because he was all those things too. She wrote about a relationship that filled each of them from a place of overflow instead of lack. For seven days Emma visualized her ideal partner, feeling in her cells all the adventures they would be going on, the snuggles and special time they would have together as if it were happening now. She also outwardly prepared for his arrival by making room for him in her home and her life. These actions showed faith in God or a higher power and proved that she was ready.

The last assignment I gave her was to forgive and send love and light to all the past relationships that she felt deceived by, the ones where she felt abandoned and not fully seen. When you send out unconditional love—when you fully forgive others and salute the divinity in them and yourself—you are sending *real* love, and real love will return to you. The divine love that is your match will come and find you.

Twenty-five days later I got an email from her. We had taken a break from our coaching because she had an overseas business trip. I assumed she was writing to tell me how it went, but what I saw instead delighted me. She had met another entrepreneur at this conference, and their souls immediately ignited. They fell in love so quickly, it felt as if they'd been assigned to one another. Their partnership was everything she'd envisioned. They were moving in together, and although he had his own home, he would be moving in with her because she had more space.

By the time I was reading her email, his clothes were in that closet, his car was in the garage, and the empty space in her king-size bed was taken.

 ## ABUNDANCE ACTION

To become a magnet for your intimate dream partner or your ideal friend, you can implement these specific actions.

1. You must become a vibrational match of what you are calling in. Watch the words and thoughts you are putting out energetically. If you claim that "all the good ones have been taken" or that "no one is there for you," the Universe will match your energy. Align your words, thoughts, and energy with what you are calling in. Statements like "My dream partner and friend is here, and I will be meeting them soon" or "I trust in the divine timing of my

ideal partner" will start creating an intentional alignment, bringing forth what you desire.

2. Write out in detail what you want to bring into your awareness with this ideal partner or friend. How do you feel with them? What are you doing together? The clearer you are, the more attuned you will become. When writing, remember to use affirmative statements like "I am," "I have," and "I choose."

3. Be the friend or partner you are seeking. You must become what you are desiring. Watch your character and your behaviors, and make sure they are aligned with what you are calling in. Forgive your past relationships that have hurt you. Forgive yourself and send divine love by saying, "I salute the divine light in you."

4. Trust. Lean back and allow the miracles of what you are intending to flow in.

PURPOSE

*noun. an intense desire or
enthusiasm for something; a person's
sense of resolve or determination*

the stories
we tell ourselves

❧

Everything can be taken from a man
but one thing: the last of the human freedoms—
to choose one's attitude in any given
set of circumstances, to choose one's own way.

— VICTOR FRANKL

One of the most potent times of uncertainty and suffering throughout human history occurred during the Holocaust. Viktor Frankl, a preeminent psychiatrist and neurologist, was incarcerated in four different Nazi concentration camps, from 1942 to 1945, while his entire family perished. He was separated from his wife, who was sent to the women's camp Bergen-Belsen, but it was his focus on her and his internal narrative that helped him survive.

When Frankl arrived at the first camp, the prisoners were separated into those who were healthy and could be put to hard labor and those who weren't strong enough to work and were therefore sent to die in the gas chambers. In *Man's Search for Meaning*, Frankl talked about suffering as being like that gas, filling the chamber no matter how large it was—just as suffering can fill the soul, no matter how great or small that suffering might be.

The concept of suffering takes on different meanings in a situation like this. The physical suffering of the beatings, vitamin deficiencies, starvation, labor, injuries, the cold—all these were present. And yet according to Frankl, "It was not the physical pain that hurt most . . . but the mental agony caused by the injustice/unreasonableness/insult of beatings . . . We had all been, or fancied ourselves to be 'somebody.' Now we were treated like complete nonentities. (The consciousness of one's inner value is anchored in higher, more spiritual things, and cannot be shaken by camp life. But how many free men, let alone prisoners, possess it?)"

One morning he was put to work digging a trench, and he was imagining a conversation with his wife, as he often did. He was losing faith, struggling to find a reason for his suffering and for the suffering of everyone around him. And in that moment, in the gray dawn light, he felt a resounding yes. There was a purpose. There was meaning. For hours after that, he hacked at the icy ground, insulted by guards, and so he once again talked with his wife in his mind. As he did, he felt that she was present with him there—they could almost touch. A bird flew down and perched on the heap of soil he had just dug up.

Frankl had this experience time and again. When he reached a moment of despair, he called for meaning, for reason, and he always found it. No matter what atrocities he suffered, nothing could take away his mind and the stories he told himself to keep going. They could do what they wanted with his body, but they couldn't touch *his soul*.

And so Frankl devoted his time in the camps to studying what allowed his fellow prisoners to survive, and his iconic findings, called logotherapy, provide a model for how we can navigate any time of uncertainty or chaos. What he found was that the people who survived the camp, regardless of their age or any other demographic or health indicators, were those who were able to make meaning of their suffering. Whether it was caring for a loved one, serving as a beacon of hope for others, or simply holding on to hope that they will one day reunite with their loved ones, those who lived for a purpose were significantly more resilient and likely to survive.

ROCK BOTTOM

The story I told myself in my teens was that I was not allowed to make mistakes. I told myself that holy, good girls didn't party, make out with boys, lie, steal, or cheat. And I obeyed every rule. I was the best, holiest rule follower, and I prided myself in this fact. My stories followed me into my early twenties, when I continued to ensure that I followed all the rules and that I was being holy. I married the boy I thought was the holiest and would take me to the Kingdom of God. I believed that good things happened to good people.

So when I wasn't happy in my marriage and had multiple surgeries and difficult pregnancies, I wondered what I was doing wrong. At first I doubled down on my goodness. I tried to be even holier. I focused more in church and buried any questions I had regarding religion or my marriage. I tried to be an even better wife, did "wifey" things, and hid the internal ache inside myself that said I was made for more. When my son passed away, I finally threw my hands in the air. The stories I was telling myself were not working anymore. More and more pain unraveled me, revealing to me that if good things happen to good people, then I must have been the baddest of the bad. I sank to my rock bottom.

Rock bottom is a magical place. It's the place where you can finally say, "I don't give two hoots anymore. I have nothing left for anyone else, so I might as well be *me.*" This place of uncertainty, chaos, and unraveling was a gift wrapped in sandpaper. I started unpacking the stories I had been told about who I *should* be, what I *should* do, and how I *should* behave. I started asking, *Is this true?*

As I dismantled what wasn't true for me, I was then able to write a new story. One where good girls are also a little wild. Good girls use their voices, are messy, and mess up. Good girls have bad days. Good girls can and will have pain, which will also become their power. I chose to see my power. I chose to see where I was suffering, and I chose a different story and meaning from that suffering. I started seeing it as a gift, and I started on a journey to find who I was. I collected my mess and made it my message.

ABUNDANCE ACTION

We are living with uncertainty. It leaves wide-open spaces for our overactive minds to kick into worst-case-scenario thinking and obsessive worrying. There is no better time than now for the world to have you in your highest purpose. To have you living in faith and creating powerful meaning from what is presenting itself to you. It is one thing to know that making meaning of your suffering helps, but it's quite another thing to actually do it. This simple but powerful process was designed by Lindsay Sukornyk, a leadership coach. It will help you survive your most challenging times and ultimately use them as an opportunity to transform and thrive. For today, you will take some time to journal about these questions.

Step One: Witness and Feel. The first step is to tap into "witness consciousness," a state in which you can experience your emotions, but you are also able to stand back and observe them. There's a common expression in the transformational space: "Name it to tame it." The best way to overcome emotions is to get them out of your mind and psyche and into the light of self-awareness. Write it out—what are you feeling?

Step Two: Acceptance. Once you have identified what you're going through, the next step is to accept the reality that you're facing. It can be hard to look at the inconvenient truths of your life, to grieve the death of dreams you may have had, or to take responsibility for a mess you may have created. However, as the Buddhists say, the root of all suffering comes from wishing that things are other than they are. In your journal, process your feelings of acceptance.

Step Three: Making Meaning. Storytelling is among the most powerful tools we hold. The narrative that we create about any situation can determine whether the circumstances are deeply destructive or whether they can fuel our expansion. Ask yourself, *What are the lessons and the blessings in this situation?* Write them out.

Step Four: Life as Art. The final step in making meaning of your suffering is to use the energy of chaos to fuel your life. If we think of any life experience as simply a flow of energy, like a thread in a tapestry that is always changing, you can use that energy to make art, whether in writing, painting, singing, dancing—whatever calls to you. Consider that your life is art. You can use the energy of any life circumstance to fuel you in your self-expression. Where can you create some art today?

bamboo

*Writing is a spiritual path. It helps you
listen to your heart, trust your inner guidance,
and live your life full-out.*

— ROBERT HOLDEN

Amanda had been doing everything right. She got up
early to put in extra hours, and she networked even when
it was uncomfortable. She made sacrifices both financial
and personal. But it was all worth it to her because she had
a dream that she truly believed in, a dream of creating
something that would make a difference in the world. She
knew in her soul that this was what she was meant to do
in this life.

After years of working and sacrificing, however, Amanda
began to feel defeated. She called up a dear friend, crying,
"I can't do this anymore. I've been working tirelessly for
years now, and I have nothing to show for it. I feel I may
need to accept that it's just not going to happen. I will have
to give up and move on."

Her friend listened, as she had listened in times past to the excitement and passion the woman had had for her dream. Her friend said, "Before you give up, promise me you'll see someone. I've heard of a wise woman who has helped many people. Maybe she has answers for you. Promise me you'll talk to her."

Amanda reluctantly agreed and made a visit. The wise woman opened her door and made a pot of tea and listened as Amanda poured out her troubles, her disappointment, and her sense of failure. And finally the wise woman said, "Let me tell you about my garden. I have a lovely garden out back, and I work in it all the time. I grow flowers and herbs and all kinds of things, and I always start from seed, so I can see the whole journey of each plant from start to finish.

"I planted this one seed of lucky bamboo, because I was in a hurry and I wanted something that would grow quickly. I'd heard that bamboo was the fastest growing plant in all the world. But I waited and I waited, and nothing happened. I watered that seed and cared for it like I care for all my plants, giving them so much love. I waited for *four years*, and nothing happened, not even a single sprout. I'd never had a plant that failed to grow, and I felt so miserable. I started to question my abilities as a gardener."

Amanda cried into her tea. "That's just how I feel!" she said. "I feel like it's all been for nothing."

The wise woman smiled and patted her hand. "I've been there," she said. "Everyone has. Come outside with me. I want to show you my garden."

Amanda wiped away her tears and followed the wise woman out into the garden, and it was as lovely and peaceful as the wise woman had described. The sweet scent of the flowers flowed on the breeze, and the hardworking honeybees hummed a soothing harmony with the rustling of the leaves.

"Come," the wise woman said, and together they walked to a tall bamboo tree that stretched up over the garden, swaying in the breeze. "I planted that seed just over four years ago," she said. "All that time I thought it wasn't doing anything down there in the ground. I didn't have anything to show for it. But the whole time it was hard at work, creating a root structure to support it. And you won't believe this, but just a few months ago, there was still nothing here. This tree grew eighty feet in just eight weeks. It had been doing everything to prepare, and when it was ready, it soared."

Amanda looked up at the bamboo tree in awe. "It doesn't seem possible," she said.

The wise woman smiled. "I know. But it is."

And so Amanda went home. She got up early the next morning, and she worked on her dream. She made phone calls and developed relationships. She lived in alignment with what she wanted to manifest in her life and in the world. And one day—not the next day, or the day after that, but soon—her dream soared.

WISDOM GREATER THAN GOOGLE

Every morning I sit down in the quiet, before any distractions can intrude. I light a candle or turn on the fireplace and get a cup of tea or warm lemon water—anything that helps me create a sense of comfort. I open my journal and ask my soul, *What would you have me know?*

When I first began this practice of soul writing, I was surprised at what came out. Some of it seemed really insignificant, and some statements caught me off guard and created a stirring in my belly. I wrote about family members, team members, places where I wasn't speaking up for what I wanted, or just random thoughts, like what needed to be done for the day.

One morning, out of nowhere, I wrote *Run Facebook ads to your Live video*. Now, at the time, Facebook Live was a new concept. Nobody was running ads to them. I knew, though, that the whole point of soul writing was to trust what came out, so I went to my marketing director and asked him to run ads for the Live video I had planned.

Let's be clear: that video was *not* my best work. I shot it on my phone in a dark kitchen, and all I was offering was a green smoothie recipe and then shared my 30-day challenge. Even so, the ads worked, and that one video got over 8 million views and promoted our program, creating hundreds of thousands of new customers, and every video we did after that had just as big an impact.

That one seemingly insignificant moment of filming in my kitchen catapulted the business. I have been soul writing ever since then. I have considered employees to hire, and I have discovered wisdom regarding my children that I would have not otherwise realized. I have written about connections I've wanted to make and then reached out and seized them.

Your internal guidance has answers. It is waiting to co-create with you. You may call this God, Source, guides, Spirit, your Soul, or something else. Call it whatever feels right for you, but tune in to it, have faith, and listen.

Soul writing means that you write down whatever comes out of your pen, with no judgment, no thinking it's off track or doesn't make sense. *Your soul knows.* There is nothing to wait for. If your situation is imperfect, that doesn't mean this isn't the time—it could mean it's the *perfect* time. Soul writing is the reminder that we don't always have to struggle or do it on our own, beating against the wall when it comes to our heart's desires. When we join our heart's desire with a divine power, in love and with inspired action, we find that there is a sacred way to move through the world—a path of steady, quiet alignment.

 ## ABUNDANCE ACTION

Over the next week, in the morning or evening, ideally when the sun rises or sets, pull out your journal. Make a ritual of it by lighting a candle or turning on the fireplace. Fire is the element of transformation. It creates a sacred, calming space. Sit in your favorite chair or go out in nature with a cup of your favorite tea or lemon water. Set your intention that you will be receiving guidance. Ask God, Source, Soul, or your higher self, "What would you have me know?" or "How can I serve and move into inspired action?"

Then write whatever comes up. Don't judge; just write. And then take one of your ideas and implement it.

If you find you are thinking about someone you haven't spoken to in a long time, reach out. Bring them their favorite food or tell them about the light you see in them. Whether you get a new idea or think about something that has been brewing in your heart for a long time, make the phone calls, do the writing, and start moving your feet in the direction of making that idea a reality. If you write about speaking up for an injustice, start getting involved on your own or with a group. Listen to the truth that is ringing inside of you.

Have the courage to move in the direction of your soul. *Your soul knows.* And when you get a nudge, act on it, and see the magic unfold.

tenacity

❧

Courage is the commitment to
begin without any guarantee of success.

— Johann Wolfgang von Goethe

When Howard Schultz was the director of marketing at Starbucks, no one really understood what a café could be, at least not in America. On a visit to Milan, Italy, Schultz saw how a café could be the center of a community, a place where people could sit and talk, read, or work. And what a far cry from drip coffee! Macchiatos, espressos, café con panna, and, of course, the beloved latte. Schultz saw what Starbucks could be, but, unfortunately, the owners at the time simply didn't share his vision.

It would have been simple enough to let the idea go, but Schultz felt so strongly about it that he left Starbucks and started his own company, Il Giornale. True to its name, it was Italian in feel, serving ice cream and paninis and playing opera music in the background.

Schultz had achieved his dream of having an Italian café, but that was not the end of the story. He wasn't through with Starbucks—or maybe Starbucks wasn't through with him. Two years after opening Il Giornale, Schultz purchased Starbucks for $3.8 million.

In Italy there was a café on every corner, and that was a big part of Schultz's vision. He blended Il Giornale's espresso offerings and community feel with the Starbucks aesthetic, purchased retail spaces all over Seattle, and then expanded outward until it became the ubiquitous caffeine utopia it is today.

Here's the thing about Howard Schultz: It's not like he had a ton of expertise in coffee, much less a ton of capital to work with. Growing up, his family had very little money and often had trouble paying the bills, particularly after his father was fired after slipping on a patch of ice while on the job as a truck driver, breaking his hip and ankle.

Schultz was the first in his family to go to college, and he did so through part-time jobs and loans. And when he got out, he was a door-to-door salesman for Xerox. He fell into coffee working for Swedish drip coffee maker Hammarplast, and it was through his work there that he met the owners of Starbucks, who eventually brought him on as marketing director.

Schultz stated, "I never set out to build a global business. I set out to build the kind of company that my father never had a chance to work for. One that treats all people with dignity."

FACEBOOK

Passion is the fuel that will inspire us, driving us toward our goals, no matter how unlikely or difficult they might be. It will keep you going when the floor falls out from underneath you. It is the tenacity and grit that you get to hold on to when all else fails.

About a year into our business, Craig and I were holding on by a thread, trying to make it work and living off the bare minimum to feed my girls. We were using Facebook as our main and pretty much only way to capture subscribers or followers and bring them onto our email list. We would give away a free delicious recipe in exchange for an email address, and we were making some progress until one day Craig came to me with tears in his eyes. We had been banned from Facebook.

He was devastated. Without Facebook there would be no leads coming in, and therefore no money and soon enough no business.

Call it intuition, grit, a farm girl up against a rock and a hard place, or whatever you want, but deep down I knew it was going to be okay and that it would all get worked out. There was not an ounce of me that felt that our dream would not be a reality, for in my heart and mind, I knew it was backed by God. I knew I was supported, and I knew this would get resolved. And when you *know*, you find a way—and we did. It took a little time, but soon enough we were back up on Facebook, and our business continued to chug along. I am thankful for that time, that moment of true *knowing* I had, which allowed us to find a solution. Since then we have gone from chugging to flying most days, and I am happy to say we've been invited to Facebook headquarters many times.

Most success stories are backed by an unquenchable passion. It is the one thing you really need to succeed, and it is always available. You don't need money to buy it, you don't need education to have it, and you don't need to know someone to attain it. It is *inside you*. It is the fire that will allow you to keep going when others tell you to stop.

 ## ABUNDANCE ACTION

If you have been wondering what your "passion and purpose" are, inquire within yourself, and write down what comes up.

What makes my heart sing?

What would I do if money wasn't an issue?

What are the activities I do that give me the feeling that time has stopped? What can I do for long periods of time without getting bored, frustrated, or tired?

Once you've answered these questions or if you know what your passion is, move in actions of faith and keep developing it. Keep placing one foot in front of the other. Follow your curiosity, paying attention to what lights you up inside. Ensure that you set aside time to pursue your passion every single day. If your passion is writing, make sure you write every day, whether it is 30, 15, or even just 10 minutes a day. If you love photography, take a picture every single day. Do not let your other tasks—or any excuses you might have—take this time from you.

You are the gatekeeper. *You* are the one who holds the key to your dreams.

conviction and convenience don't live on the same block

❧

When I look inside and see that
I am nothing, that is wisdom. When I look outside
and see that I am everything, that is love.
And between these two, my life flows.

— Sri Nisargadatta Maharaj

Abraham Lincoln is arguably our most beloved president, and much of our love for him comes from the knowledge of how much he struggled and yet remained tenacious. Every time Lincoln faced an obstacle, he overcame it. He failed at his first business at the age of 21. He lost his first legislative race the following year. He failed at his second business two years after that. At age 26 he lost his first love and had a nervous breakdown. After his recovery, at the age of 34, he went back into politics . . . but he lost that congressional race. And the one after that. Next, in his mid- to late forties, he tried for the Senate . . . but he lost two senatorial races.

Yet throughout his life, Lincoln remained steadfast. With a childhood background as a farmer, he worked hard and became a self-taught lawyer. His passion for justice led him to denounce slavery when he was running for Senate, calling the institution a violation of our most basic tenets: "This government cannot endure, permanently half slave and half free." All this dedication paid off, and he was elected President of the United States at age 52.

His election as President sent the nation into war. He knew this was a possibility, but he believed so strongly in his convictions that he ran anyway and won by a slim margin. After his inauguration he did everything he could to bind the nation back together—everything, that is, short of renouncing abolitionism. While the Confederate leader Jefferson Davis was a West Point graduate, had fought with honors in the Mexican-American War, and had been secretary of war, Lincoln had very little tactical experience. What Lincoln had developed in himself was an unquenchable and creative spirit, making him think outside the box as commander in chief.

Lincoln never lost sight of what truly mattered. He gripped the country with both hands, holding it together as it tried to wrench itself apart. He had the vision and the moral certainty to know that slavery simply had to end, and that this was, indeed, the only way for the United States to move forward as one country. When the war finally ended, there was devastation on both sides, but Lincoln was determined to bring the South back with open arms. It wasn't easy, and it wasn't popular. Lincoln changed the country and the lives of its citizens, starting us on the path of healing and coming together, with a loving embrace for all people.

RUNNER

As I've said, I come from a family of runners. From the moment my oldest brother could run, I was dragged to races all over the state. The smell of sweat and triumph from the rides home became the scent of our old brown Maverick. I started running when I was 10 years old. It was the way I processed the world. My emotions would stir, and since I didn't know how to handle what was brewing, I would run. I would run the emotions out of my cells and out of my system. I would run multiple times per week. Once high school started, I ran to compete with others, but mostly to compete with the noise in my head.

I was looking for something deeper within myself. I wanted to quiet the internal ache. I needed to feel something, to know there was something beyond the pain, the fatigue, the deep voice telling me to quit.

Running has taught me about the evolution of growth, passion, and persistence with my businesses, intimate relationships, parenting, friends, and my personal spiritual journey. In most of the races or long runs that I have done, there is a pattern.

First: *The anticipation.* In running there is a universal truth: *You aren't looking back.* You are only looking forward. And you will start the race. And once you start, you will *feel* it all.

Second: *The start.* It feels good. You feel like a badass. You have the wind in your hair and a feeling of euphoria sweeping over you because it's just the beginning and you feel strong.

Third: *The climb.* When you are three-fourths of the way through the race, it starts to suck. Your legs and lungs are tired, and the feel-good feelings are gone. The voice in your head says, *You think this is fun? Why did you sign up for this? Rest. Better yet, stop. You are not trained enough. You are not equipped enough. You simply are not enough.*

Fourth: *The reprieve.* If you get past this onslaught and continue with your passion and grit, you get a moment where the wind is back in your hair. You may feel a slight downhill. Your legs get to coast, and you feel like you are back in the race. You get your hopes up.

Fifth: *The last hill.* This hill is the suckiest of all because you're caught off guard. You thought the pain and suck was over and you let go of your grit and stamina and put your shield down. This is where you come against yourself. This is where your mean inner self will rear its ugly head. This is the part where your mind tries to take over your body. To tell you that you are going to get injured and you will never recover. This is the part in the race where you will be most tempted to slow down, walk, or simply quit.

Sixth: *Victory.* This phase is for those who did not quit on the last hill. You become your own hero, your biggest champion, and you use your pain as fuel. You tell your mind to take a hike and start chanting, *I am fantastic. I feel great. I am a champion. I am a finisher. I am enough. I choose my story.* In the distance, you see the finish line. You can taste it, smell it, feel it. The deep, insatiable itch is about to get scratched. The goose bumps begin to pop all over your body as a surge of endorphins consumes your cells from your toes to your head.

And then you cross the finish line.

What I know is that you are more equipped than you think. You are more supported than you know, and you are more loved and destined than you realize. Be courageous enough to run the race when no one is cheering. When you feel tired. When you feel like giving up.

But please, for the love of all things holy, run the damn race.

 ## ABUNDANCE ACTION

As you grow and continue on your journey in this life, your next right move will shift. The only moment you have is the here and now. What at this moment is brewing inside your cells? Is there a deeper knowing of what that next right move is? Here are a few specific questions you can ask yourself right now:

1. **What is true about you today that would make the seven- or eight-year-old version of yourself cry?** When I was younger, I

loved being with animals. I would sit for hours outside with my family's herd of sheep and sing to them. I would comb the horses' manes and play fetch with the dogs. As I got older and grew into being a mother and running a business, I made up a story that I didn't like dogs and that I didn't need pets. They were messy and would take up precious time taking care of them. Then I asked myself this question and realized that the little girl within would cry if she thought that her older self would never have animals around her. We ended up getting a dog, and she became the angel in our lives. She was there for my children in their lonely, dark days, and with me in mine. Many walks with her out in nature have stirred ideas in my mind that have been catalysts for massive abundance.

2. **What makes you forget to eat or go to the bathroom?** When I travel, I am filled with the smells, newness, and richness of a region and its people. It is when I am traveling that I receive the greatest insights about myself, my purpose, and my business. What is your thing? Once you have discovered it, figure out how you can do more of it. Once you start doing more of what lights you up and makes time stand still, you will become a powerful magnet to all that lies in your heart.

3. **If you were going to die in one month, what would you do each day, and what would you want to be remembered for?** This is a deep question and one I encourage everyone to face. None of us know when our last breath will be taken. Truly stepping into the idea and feeling of your death will allow you to see and feel what really matters to you, and what you would *love* to be doing. It takes out all the drama and illusion of social media and making *x* amount of money, and it puts your focus where it belongs: on impact, significance, love, and joy.

zone of genius

❧

It's hard to read the label
when you're inside the box of your life.

— ANONYMOUS

There once was a girl who always knew in every fiber of her being that she could achieve anything in the world she wanted to. All she had to do was choose something and focus, and she would succeed at it. One day, she sat down in front of a blank canvas and began to paint. Each stroke was more perfect than the last, slowly and gracefully converging to form a flawless masterpiece. When she finished the painting, she stared proudly at her work and smiled.

After many beautiful masterpieces, she began to feel anxious. She knew that she could do anything in the world, anything at all—so what was she doing spending her time pushing paint around?

She looked away from her masterpiece and went outside for a walk in the moonlight. And as she walked, she thought, and walked some more.

Should she practice medicine? Design buildings? Teach children? She was utterly stumped at what she should do next. She didn't notice the clouds and stars trying to signal to her—she was too preoccupied with the important decision she was trying to make.

So she kept walking. And thinking. And walking. Twenty-five years later, the girl began to cry. She had been walking for so long, feeling so enamored by the endless possibilities of everything she *could* do that she hadn't actually done any of them. So the girl, who was no longer a girl, purchased some paint and canvas, went to a nearby park, and began to paint. One stroke gracefully led into the next, just as it had done so many moons ago. And she smiled and continued to paint through the day and into the night. She had finally made a decision. And there was still time to revel in the magic of life. She had learned, at last, that life wasn't about possibility. Anything was possible. Life was about making the decision to do something that moves you.

PICKUP TRUCK

Children are often better at identifying their genius than adults. Their sense of play and simple desire to do what they enjoy helps them see and feel what they want to do "when they grow up."

When I was a little girl, I used to ride between my parents in our truck when we would go into town or up to the mountains. I would chatter away with them, sharing my dreams. I told them I was going to bring women to the mountains and help them feel love for themselves through the love of nature. I told them I wanted to help millions of women feel their power. My parents would nod and smile, but I *knew*. I felt this truth in myself as strongly as the heat of the leather seat of the truck under my skin.

My 10-year-old self was wise and in tune with her soul. Today I *love* what I get to do. I bring millions of women back to themselves, back to nature, and help them rise up in the power of their voices and knowing.

We live with this story in our society that tells us that something has to be hard or not fun to be worthy of money. To be a job, there has to be drudgery. If we were to make a living by doing the thing that's peaceful and fun— something we would do whether we were getting paid or not—that would feel like fraud.

That story simply isn't true.

This thread in you that brings you joy and makes time stop, allowing you to be in the present moment, is your gift and possibly your gift to the world. You were given this thing that feels so easy, so fun, because that's what you were *meant* to do. There is, for each person, a perfect self-expression. There is a place that you can only fill, something you can do that no one else can, which is your destiny. You may not know right away what this is, for it is deep within you, waiting for you to call it forth. The perfect plan includes health, wealth, love, and perfect self-expression.

My wish is for you to have the courage to live out your genius, your superpower. To honor the gifts that lie in you. To trust that as you step into more joy, more ease and flow, that you will know that you are serving at your highest level.

ABUNDANCE ACTION

You might be wondering, *How do I really know what my genius is?* Genius can be channeled. It is not just for the smartest or the most talented; instead it shows itself in those who operate in their soul, with a connection to the divine. It is chosen by the divine.

Here are some ways for you to uncover the genius inside:

Step One: First, declare your intentions to God, the Universe, infinite intelligence, or Source every day: "Infinite Spirit, open the way for the divine design of my life to manifest; let the genius within me now be released; let me see clearly the perfect plan."

Step Two: Make a list of the five people you admire the most. These may be people you know personally or have read or heard about. They can be alive or deceased. Next write out the attributes, qualities, or characteristics you love and see in them. Once you have done this for all five people, circle only the similar attributes. Write out these qualities on a separate sheet of paper. Add the phrase "I am" before the quality. These qualities you see in these individuals live inside of you.

Step Three: Read these "I am" qualities every day.

Step Four: Take a look at your calendar, and for the next two weeks, make sure you schedule in some activities or experiences that will allow you to use these talents and qualities.

PROSPERITY

noun. a successful, flourishing, or thriving condition, especially in financial respects; good fortune

your money story

❧

All that we are is
the result of what we have thought.

— BUDDHA

Not only did Alyssa Nobriga think she didn't have enough—she didn't think she *was* enough. She would stand outside fancy stores like Prada or Cartier, wanting to go in and look, but she wouldn't feel worthy of entering. She imagined they would look at her and know instantly that she didn't have the means.

Alyssa was attending grad school and making $16K a year. She was sleeping on a friend's futon in Santa Monica and living off protein bars. Everyone she knew was 10 years older and much further along in their careers.

She felt less than. A lot less than. This was reinforced when friends would want to get together at restaurants, and she would go and not eat anything, saying she wasn't hungry, when in truth she couldn't afford it.

With time she began to unravel her self-worth from her net worth. This practice took internal work, along with some painful truth telling.

When Alyssa would get caught up in feelings of worthlessness and not being good enough, she would sit with that feeling. She wouldn't let herself tell a story around it; she would just sit with it and really feel it. She would question the limiting beliefs that led to those feelings, and hold them up to the light, revealing them to be the flimsy untruths they were. And then she would embrace and feel compassion for herself for feeling that way and getting caught up in the comparison game.

In conjunction with her inner work, Alyssa did the outer work necessary to build her career. She said yes to the opportunities that presented themselves, even if they were intimidating or downright terrifying. Alyssa also took the step of investing in herself and her business. She used up any free cash she had and signed up for business and mindset coaching and worked on her money story, along with practical business tools to help her succeed.

The investment she made in herself was priceless because it allowed her to truly see that no matter what happened to her—the economy tanking, a relationship not working out, a crisis in the family—she knew that she could support herself while at the same time being of service to the world. It was the greatest security she could ever have.

GAMBLING

I was raised believing that the lottery was a form of gambling, and it was frowned upon to rely on anything outside yourself for your financial success. So when I bought my first lotto ticket in my twenties, I was discreet, and I didn't tell anyone. It was as if I had done something that was forbidden or unworthy. Over a million dollars was at play, and I was salivating with hope.

As the numbers were revealed, I watched as my hope was slashed within seconds. No match.

I then looked up lottery winners. Their lives must be amazing! But with each person I read about, I found a common denominator. Even with millions falling upon them, by five years, most had lost everything and were back living the lifestyle they had before winning, and 70 percent of them went bankrupt—worse off than before they were gifted with cash. I yelled at the screen when I read case after case. How was this possible? How could someone who just came across millions of dollars lose it all so quickly? How could such a high percentage become worse off than before?

Over the years, I dove deeper into this phenomenon. On the outside you find that most of these individuals turned to the wrong people, often friends of a friend, for advice on how to handle their money, instead of seeking a professional or an attorney. They gave large sums of it away to family members asking for help, and they ended up quitting their jobs and buying items that had no long-term value, like cars, homes, and endless vacations and accessories. This grandiose way of life spun them out of control until they had nothing left—no job and no dream, just a mounting hill of debt.

The internal phenomenon that is happening to most lotto winners is caused by their subconscious beliefs. Receiving this newfound wealth does not necessarily align with their feelings of worthiness around receiving it. Their belief around the amount of money they feel they deeply deserve has not been fully cultivated.

There have been many studies looking at lotto winners who won large sums of money overnight, and they showed extreme levels of spending followed by crashes of anxiety, withdrawal, and feelings of loneliness. Our money story, or belief around what we feel we deserve, affects us internally through emotion as well as externally by what we allow to remain in our investments and bank accounts.

Having large sums of money overnight is a dream for most of us, as is accumulating it by working hard in pursuit of our passion. I believe having enough and having more than enough is our birthright. Your only job is to align your worth. Look at your money story and your worthiness to receive it. When we put in the honesty and willingness to work on our internal business—our worthiness of wealth—then the financial abundance will be able to flow in.

 ## ABUNDANCE ACTION

In each moment, you have a choice: to question your limiting beliefs and get free or to remain stuck. Every time you catch yourself in these beliefs, try to weaken them and break their pattern. You'll wake up out of the trance of scarcity.

You are more than worthy, and you are more than you could ever imagine yourself to be.

These journal prompts from Alyssa Nobriga will help you unravel the money blocks that may be standing in the way of experiencing more freedom and abundance in your life.

1. What did I learn about money from my parents or primary caregivers?

2. If I make more money, I'm afraid that . . .

3. If I fully knew my own worth, what would my life be like? What would I do or stop doing?

4. Do I feel worthy, deep in my gut, in all the fibers of my being, of having financial freedom? If the answer is no, this is a great time to write out the reasons why and list all the reasons why you should be abundant financially.

YOUR FINANCIAL COMEBACK PLAN

Access an entire financial blueprint to getting your feet back under you when you've lost it all here:

www.EmbraceAbundanceBook.com/resources

the obstacle
is the way

❧

A river cuts through a rock
not because of its power but its persistence.

— JIM WATKINS

There was once a little girl with an extreme fear of heights. She had slipped and fallen off the edge of a short cliff when she was very young. She wasn't badly hurt—it could have been much worse!—but the memory of sliding over the edge loomed over her and made it difficult for her to cope with everyday life. Her fear was so powerful that she had to crawl up any stairs that didn't have railings. It was debilitating, not to mention embarrassing.

But the hardest part was that her siblings were daredevils. They loved roller coasters and skiing and doing all kinds of things that this little girl couldn't overcome her fear of and participate in. She felt horribly left out, especially when they were all having a great time while she just sat and watched.

One family vacation, her siblings wanted to go zip-lining through the forest. Now, the little girl loved forests more than anything and hated the thought of missing out on this experience, but it was just so *high*.

The little girl could have stayed at the hotel, but she decided to go.

When the zip-line guides were strapping her in, she was shaking. She watched her brother make the first leap, and he screamed with joy as he soared from tree to tree.

She watched her sister go, and her father, and then her mother, until she was standing alone, just her and the guide.

She started to panic. She began crying and shaking, her heart racing as her body became numb.

The guide put his arm around her. "Hey," he said gently. "You don't have to do this, you know. We can take you back down, and you can wait for your family there."

The little girl's mother yelled from the platform, waving him off.

"She's panicking," the guide yelled. "I think we need to call this off, okay?"

"Leave her alone!" the mother yelled back.

The guide was taken aback. "I was just . . ."

The mother forcefully waved him off again.

The little girl sniffled. The guide watched her, feeling sorry for her, as she walked to the edge. She shut her eyes tight and stood there for some time. Then she took a deep breath and opened her eyes again. She leaped off the platform and soared. She felt the wind in her hair as she watched her beloved trees and the beauty of a canopy that could only be seen from the sky, in flight.

And when she landed, she went straight into her mother's arms, and her entire family surrounded her with their love and their pride.

This little girl's mother knew what our creator, God, the Universe, and Source know—when we overcome our own obstacles, it can lead us to our greatest joys. When faced with adversity, we must struggle, oftentimes on our very own, so we can understand our true strength. And we must fall so that we know we can get up 1,001 times. It is who we are in the face of adversity that defines our character.

WASHING MACHINE

When I had lost my son and was going through financial ruin, divorce, and being a single parent all around the same time, I was met with my true self. Most days I felt like I couldn't breathe and prayed that the spinning and sucking for air would just *stop*. I wondered if I was ever going to live out my dreams, if I was ever going to pull out from the depression and the brain fog that drowned me in darkness every day. I tried to figure out how I could be my biggest rescuer since there were only me, my faith, and my creator. And so in my darkest days, I found my courage, my strength, and my life, and I eventually crawled out of the washing machine and turned it off.

Looking back, I can honestly say I am so grateful now that I went through that time. I now know that no matter what crisis, chaos, or downfall hits me, I have a deep internal strength. I can get through anything. It's not going to be fun, and it's not always going to be pretty, but I know without a shadow of a doubt that I can get through it. There is no darkness we can enter without being met by love.

 # ABUNDANCE ACTION

As we step into more abundance financially, we will have to face some of the emotions or stories around lack. To create a new pattern in the brain and ultimately in your reality, begin by writing out all the messy, dark, painful emotions you may be experiencing. You can do this around your finances as well as any area of your life. Now, this isn't going to be fun to write, but have your list go on and on until you have exhausted these feelings.

And then write the opposite next to these negative emotions. This is the truth of the courage within you, the truth that you need to know and believe. Read this list every day, filling up your mind and soul with the direction you are choosing to go in.

I feel broken.	I am enough.
I am angry about my lack of money.	I feel peace knowing abundance is coming.
I'm a financial ruin.	I am a financial success.

I am weak.	I am strong.
I don't feel like I matter.	I matter and my dreams are important.
I am frustrated.	I am motivated.
I've let everyone down, including myself.	I am making a difference in my life and in the lives of my family members.

vision

Nothing happens unless first a dream.

— Carl Sandburg

When Hannah was young, she liked to play dress-up. She was particularly obsessed with Jane Austen and the clothes women wore in the Regency period in England. It all seemed so elegant, so beautiful, and so much fun. She begged her grandmother to teach her to sew, and by the time she was in high school, she was really good at it. She could make entire gowns from scratch, using vintage patterns and designs she had created herself. She was even fashioning corsets and petticoats.

But when she graduated high school, she went to college to learn to be a dentist. There were a lot of dentists in her family, and she knew it would make a good living. It took a lot of studying, and she didn't have as much time for sewing as she wanted. Whenever she had a break, she worked on a new dress, but she wasn't able to get to it as often as she wanted. And as time went by, she noticed that her spirits were low. She was doing well in school, and she knew when she got out she'd have a successful career, but she missed her sewing machine. She missed her gowns, her corsets, and her petticoats. Sometimes she dressed up in them just for fun, sitting around in a tea gown while studying molars.

One day a friend dropped by while she was all dressed up, and her friend was amazed. "You *made* this? That's incredible! I've never seen anything like it! Would you make me one?"

Hannah had never made a dress for anyone else. "I don't know," she said.

"I'll pay you! I'd really love one. How much would you charge?"

Hannah hesitated. The fabric was expensive, and sewing a gown like this took a very long time. "You're not going to want to pay me," she said wryly. "It'd be like $300."

Her friend beamed. "That's totally worth it! Maybe I'll get one for my mom too—she loves Jane Austen!"

So Hannah made her friend a dress, and she made one for her friend's mother too. And then other friends asked, and soon enough people she didn't even know were eager to pay her to do what she loved. Before she even realized it, she had a business. It seemed unthinkable—but there it was. She dropped out of dentistry school and opened an Etsy shop. It was terrifying at first, and there were some hiccups—some orders were late because she couldn't get the fabric she needed, and some periods were so slow she didn't know if the business would make it. But as she continued to stay in the dream of what she loved, it seemed to flourish, and the dress business expanded into making costumes for film and theater. It had seemed impossible, impractical; just a dream—but Hannah took the leap of faith and made her dream a reality.

DREAM MAPPING

When I was a single mother, with $47 to my name, sleeping on a mattress on the floor with tin foil on the TV antenna to get three channels and borrowing Wi-Fi from the neighbors through the walls, I had nowhere to go but up.

I didn't have connections or money to borrow, but I did have a dream in my heart. I had learned about the power of writing down your dreams and reading them every day. I wrote out in great detail exactly how I saw my life in one year and three years, and the big, audacious goals I had at each goalpost. I was specific down to the color of my car, what the interior looked like, and how my home felt and looked. I saw my clientele so vividly in my mind and how I was helping them and the way my product or service was making them feel. I wrote down what my health was like, what I was eating, and how I felt in my skin. I wrote out my favorite date ideas with which to stay connected with my future partner, and all the loving things he would do for me and I for him. I wrote out all the ways I was going to give back through charitable donations. I wrote my hairy, scary dreams of how I was changing lives, including my own.

Looking at that paper every day created a shift in my brain. Everything in my external world started to match up with my internal dreams I had put down in my journal.

What you think, you become.

ABUNDANCE
ACTION

When you put your vision down on paper, look at it every single day, and *feel* the emotions you would experience, just as if that vision were already a reality, your mind begins rewiring to find a solution, steps, connections, and opportunities to line up with the feeling you are creating. This is where the magic sauce is. By seeing it in your mind, writing it down, feeling it in your body, and getting into action, you will become aware of these dreams presenting themselves in your reality.

Get yourself into a space where you feel inspired and can focus and relax into writing. Start journaling in detail about these seven main areas of your life. Be as specific as you can, and do not worry about the *how*.

Relationships: What does your relationship look and feel like with your children, your significant other, yourself, your family, and your friends?

Health: How do you feel and look in your body? What is your health like? What are you eating or doing to be the healthiest version of you?

Finances: How much money do you make? How much do you have saved up? What home do you live in, where do you live, and what car are you driving?

Spirituality: What does your mental and spiritual health look and feel like? How do you honor yourself? How do you stay connected with a higher power?

Career: What is your passion and purpose, and what are you doing to help others? How long do you work and where? What does your typical day look like?

Philanthropy: In what ways do you give back? How much and to whom?

Fun: What do you do for fun? What vacations do you take and where? What do you do each day that lights you up?

Each day, read what you wrote, and watch as your dreams appear in your life.

more than enough

The earth is generous and abundant in its giving.
It's we human beings with our fear of scarcity that
end up blocking the flow of abundance.

— PHILIP CHIRCOP

David got up every day at 5 A.M. And every day he woke
up sweating, his heart racing. He made himself a cup of
tea and tried not to wake the rest of his household. His
wife and daughter woke up around 7 A.M., and David
headed into work by 8 A.M. His office was in Manhattan,
and his commute was 50 minutes each way. He worked
hard and he did well. He had a large, beautiful house with
four bedrooms, five living rooms, and an office. He took
his family on vacation every year, and invariably they went
to places as far from the city as possible. They went to cab-
ins on lakes, hiked in the mountains, and camped in the
forests. Every weekend they could get away, they drove out
to the countryside. David's daughter loved animals and his
wife loved quiet.

But by Monday morning they were back to the noise
of the city.

Then one day they decided there had to be a change. They finally began to listen to their internal voices, the ones that had been clamoring for a simpler, quieter life. A life that didn't require long commutes, a large home to manage, or the desire to run off to the wilderness whenever there was a break. David quit his job. They sold their house and donated most of their stuff—including David's suits—and moved halfway across the country. They bought a house that was only 900 square feet but felt like home.

They traded in fancy restaurants for raising chickens and grew vegetables. Instead of shopping they tended to the lemon trees and got a dog who sat at David's feet while he worked on their front porch in the sunshine. And the hustle and bustle of the city was exchanged for three acres of soothing silence. David still got up at five in the morning every day, but now it was to take his dog on a walk to watch the sunrise.

ABUNDANCE CODE

My family was by no means well off, and certainly not wealthy. I grew up on a farm, surrounded by hundreds of sheep, four dogs, and at least 30 chickens. Those were my friends, and I felt like the luckiest little girl in the world to be able to head down to the pasture to play with my friends. We had what we needed and had food on the table, faith, love, and each other. Despite this wonderful upbringing, I took on a story that money was hard to attain.

When I became a mom of two young girls, my understanding of wealth began to take on a new meaning. Not only did I want to provide financially for them, I wanted to create a new pattern around women making money and their sense of self-worth, both for myself and for my daughters' generation. I wanted to crack the code of an abundant mindset. I was on a quest.

I started diving into the stories of people who grew up as I did, without a lot of money but able to acquire it through shifting their mental stories. And I discovered there was a formula. Each of them looked at the limiting beliefs they held around money and then found new affirmations they could say every day around abundance and wealth so that they could change their subconscious and conscious beliefs about money and their worth. They took tenacious action every single day, doing the necessary tasks to make their beliefs match up with their reality.

I modeled myself after them. I recognized that I had limiting beliefs about the amount of money that would be appropriate for me to make and that I thought that people who made a lot of money were greedy, stingy, stuck-up, and so forth. I started with writing down all these limiting beliefs.

Money doesn't grow on trees.

Wealthy people are greedy.

You can't make a lot of money and still be a good mom.

If you make a lot of money, you'll be neglecting your children.

If you make a lot of money, you're not humble.

If you make a lot of money, you won't have true friends.

If you have a lot of money, everyone will ask you for things.

Then I looked at these limiting beliefs and asked myself if they were true. None of them were. None of them were things I actually believed within myself; they were ideas that had been placed upon me.

So I wrote down new beliefs, and I still read them every day.

I am increasing in abundance, success, and love every day, and I am inspiring my children and myself to do the same.

I am increasing in abundance whether I'm working, sleeping, or playing.

When good people make money, they can do more good.

I am deserving of wealth. I am an abundant being. My creator is pouring over me.

Over time I noticed that as I worked on my abundance mindset, things began to shift. Successful business ideas started flowing in my mind. I began to get hits of inspiration for who to connect with as I stepped more and more into my purpose, and more and more into the things that lit me up and sparked my curiosity. I was able to offer more value to others and received more financial stability in return.

An abundance mindset will guide you to make the most of the money and experiences you have. It will allow you to notice *all* that is around you. It will allow you to notice the miracles.

An abundance mindset creates freedom.

Freedom to breathe.

Freedom to allow.

Freedom to see what is in front of you.

Freedom to know that you have within you all that you need.

 ## ABUNDANCE ACTION

The more time you spend in front of a screen, the worse you probably feel. Oftentimes scrolling through social media only serves to remind you of what you don't have. Advertisers get you to spend money on things you don't need or really want, and the whole experience can make you feel as though you are not enough just as you are. You imagine that if you have this or that, you will be happier, prettier, or more successful.

Make an action plan to turn off the TV and social media for today and the rest of the week. Free yourself from the stories that others place upon you about success, happiness, and worth. Spend time out in nature alone. Go for a walk, hike, bike, or sit in silence.

Write out what you really want. What truly lights you up and why? Don't think about what you've been told *should* light you up—what is true *for you*? For example, when we claim we want money, often the truth is that we want what we think money will give us: love, freedom, and time exploring the world. Be crystal clear about the deeper *why* of creating abundance. What will make you feel abundant and why?

Once you have written what you really want, take 5 to 10 minutes feeling these feelings as if you have the things you desire right now. As you feel this abundance, you will become the attractor and the vibrational match of what you desire. Feel freedom and deep unconditional love. As you experience these emotions, you become a magnet, bringing the essence of that experience into your physical reality.

the river
of abundance

❦

Your fortune is not something to find but to unfold.

— Eric Butterworth

The martial arts master eyed his students as they ran through their drills. They flowed from kick to block to punch and around again, smoothly and in sync, like a dance. Except one. This student was talented and strong, and had the potential for excellent form, but he was distracted. His timing was off, his movements were not precise, and his balance was uncertain.

At the end of the session, the master called the young man over to him. The student hung his head, frustration evident in the strain in his shoulders and the clench in his fists. "I'm sorry, master," he said. "No matter how hard I try, I cannot execute my technique as you have taught us. The others are able to follow your instructions perfectly, but I cannot. I have failed you."

The master laid a hand on the young man's shoulder. "Come with me," he said. They walked in silence, leaving the courtyard and venturing through the woods until they came to the river that ran through a gully, shadowed by the trees. They descended to the little bridge that ran over the river. Still the master said nothing, and he and his student watched the water move in eddies around the rocks that formed the riverbed. They saw how the river twisted and turned along the shoreline. Some areas were deep, while other areas were shallow.

Finally the master spoke. "Do you see how the water reaches the rocks? It does not smash itself against them but instead flows over and around them, and then moves on to flow around the next rock, and the next, never losing its way. Do you see how the river is not straight? It twists and turns to create a more efficient path. You must become like the river. When you move, move with flow. Be persistent and create new routes along your journey by twisting and turning. There are times to be deep and other times to be light. Trust in your journey. Each river is different, just like each student. Each day creates a new experience to move gracefully along the obstacles that present themselves."

The student watched the river for a moment longer and then nodded his understanding. At practice the next day, he breathed and flowed, feeling the spirit of the river, moving in eddies with the other students, with a sense of lightness and renewed focus.

RAPIDS

I can count on one hand the number of times we went out to eat at a restaurant as a family when I was a little girl. It is still etched in my mind as a day of excitement when we went to the local A&W to get burgers. And while we never went to Disneyland, to water parks, or on elaborate family vacations, the one thing we did do was river rafting. We invested in a boat, oars, and life jackets so that we could enjoy this sport as a family.

The Salmon River provided class 3 and 4 rapids, and I loved to sit at the very front of the raft, holding on to the ropes as we dove into the deep rapids, water spilling over the sides. I would scream with delight, reveling in the euphoria of that fine line between mortality and surrender.

Every day, I try to get next to a river to watch and learn from it. A river is constantly flowing. Even in the depths of winter, there is always movement beneath the sheets of ice. In the times of my deepest pain, I would cry next to a river and watch my tears fall into the water to be carried away. In the times of my deepest hope, I would stand at the river's edge and declare the truth of what I was stepping into—abundance in love, abundance in finance, and abundance in service and showing up as my truest self. I declared it to the river, who carried it away.

A river flows where it will. Whether you are in an inner tube, on a boat, or simply floating on your back, the river is the one in control. You don't get to decide which direction it's going to go—you're just along for the ride, trusting the river to take you to a safe place, enjoying the adventure of the journey.

Our thoughts are like rivers and ultimately the deepest dreams of our manifestation. So many of us are trying to paddle upstream, working against the flow, by declaring the things we do *not* want. For example, if we're in ill health, we say, "I am not doing well. I feel sick." What if you were instead to say, "I am stepping into great health," or "I trust my body. It knows how to heal and align"? This would allow you to travel *with* the river of abundance rather than fighting against it.

The same is true for financial abundance. "I just can't catch a break." "The bills are rolling in." "I want to be wealthy." These statements are paddling upstream.

"I am financially secure." "I live in an abundant world." "Everything I need is within me." "I am aware of the opportunities for wealth." These statements are floating downstream.

If you want to step into more abundance in all areas of life, watch your thoughts and your words. You are the artist of your life. Your words are your paintbrush, and your life is the canvas. You get to decide what you paint, and your words are powerful tools for creation. When you learn to use these tools with awareness, you can make your life's history with your words. The words you speak have the magic and power of creation. They produce an image, an idea, a feeling, or an entire story. For example, if you say the word *dog*, your mind will conjure an image of a dog, but if you say two words together, like *friends forever*, a whole movie can appear in your mind.

Your words become extensions of you. Are you declaring the thing you want? Or are you declaring what you do not want?

Declare where your highest self is going. Make it a daily habit to speak what is actually happening in the highest realm: "I am financially abundant. I am healthy. I am vibrant. I am sexy. I am loved. I have many friends. I am steady. I am calm. I am peaceful."

Your thoughts and your words determine your future. We need to get in the boat, speak the truth of our destination, and then sit back and enjoy the ride. Surrender to the magic of the river. Stay in the positivity of what you are manifesting, paddling with the current, going with the flow, and staying in joy, laughing as the waves crash over the sides.

ABUNDANCE ACTION

For one day take inventory of all your thoughts and your words. Don't judge them—just notice. What is the language you are speaking outwardly to others, and what is the language you are speaking internally to yourself? The first step is always awareness. Once you are aware, you can begin to change.

Next write the opposite of your negative, upstream thoughts, using the words *I am*. These two words can have the most life-altering power of any and all other words in the world. They are the words of the divine, of infinite intelligence. They are yours and yours only. No one can say "I am" for you.

When you notice yourself moving against the flow, write down an abundance statement that counters it, the truth of the evolution of your soul, the truth of where you're going. Ensure your affirmation is carefully worded and that it is satisfying to your conscious mind. Write them all down, and then visit them every day so that they pull you into the flow of the river.

Sample Statements:

It takes me a long time to learn new things. I am a slow learner.	I am divinely intelligent. I am quick-minded.
I don't have any real, *true* friends.	I am attracting fun, loving friendships.
I get anxious a lot. I feel like I am weird and don't fit in.	I am calm. I am unique and people enjoy being around me.
I am hard to love. I get angry easily.	I am deserving of love. I am getting more patient every day.
I am not a good mother.	I am a great mother.
I feel tired and sick.	I am healing. I trust in the process of life and my body's ability to heal.
Money is hard to get.	I am financially abundant. Wealth is my birthright.

PATHWAY TO PROSPERITY

It's time to embrace your financial abundance. Print out these prosperity pages for additional resources, exercises, and guidance on how you can bring more prosperity into your and your family's lives:

www.EmbraceAbundanceBook.com/resources

GIVE BACK

*verb. to provide help or assistance
to others in appreciation of one's own
success or good fortune*

legacy

♥

Legacy is not leaving something for people.
It's leaving something in people.

— PETER STROPLE

Scott Harrison grew up in the suburbs. He was a happy kid, and his parents were happy too—until one day everything changed. When Scott was four years old, his mom collapsed on the bedroom floor. They had just moved into a new house, and unbeknownst to them, there was a carbon monoxide leak. Luckily, Scott's mother survived, but her immune system was forever compromised. Perfumes, dust, and all kinds of irritants were severely harmful to her. She had to wear a mask all the time and was often hooked up to oxygen.

Scott's childhood was over. He was no longer a kid; he was now a caregiver for his mother. He cooked, did laundry, and was helpful in every way. But when he turned 18, he rebelled. He moved to New York City and became a nightclub promoter, which basically meant getting paid to drink. This lifestyle took its toll. Soon he was smoking two packs of cigarettes a day and was out drunk almost every single night. He was gambling, going to strip clubs, and did just about every drug except heroin.

He started feeling horrible about himself, sick inside and out. He felt spiritually and emotionally bankrupt.

One day he'd had enough. He took a year off, intending to serve others instead of himself. He sent applications to humanitarian organizations, but he was denied. Because of his history, they wouldn't even let him volunteer. Finally one organization agreed to take him on as a volunteer—*if* he paid them $500 a month.

Scott handed over his credit card. He traveled the world on a hospital ship, and he worked as their photojournalist. One day more than 5,000 people came for the ship's services. Some had walked for miles and miles. There were too many of them, and Scott held a camera, crying, as they turned thousands of people away.

He wanted to do more than just watch. Scott spent more and more time out in the villages, and he discovered the reason for so much sickness—many of the people he met had no clean drinking water. One in ten people in the world can't get clean water. Their most basic health needs are not being met, and they are getting sick and dying. Dirty water is responsible for more deaths in the world than war.[1]

When Scott's time on the hospital ship was over, he put his skills as a nightclub promoter to work—he threw

---

1 "Unsafe Water Kills More People than War, Ban Says on World Day," UN News, United Nations, March 22, 2010, https://news.un.org/en/story/2010/03/333182-unsafe-water-kills-more-people-war-ban-says-world-day.

a party. This one party raised enough money to dig wells and supply an entire village with clean water.

This was the beginning of Charity: Water, a nonprofit organization that brings clean drinking water to countries in need. So far Charity: Water has helped over 11 million people in 29 countries. They partner with experienced local organizations who cut through bureaucratic red tape and make sure the water gets where it's supposed to go. They ensure that all donations they receive go toward clean water, as opposed to office overhead or advertising. Charity: Water is a model of sustainable philanthropy and legacy.

A DRIVER AND A LITTLE BOY

When I was pregnant with Hap, I had complications and rushed to the hospital. I left the next day with empty arms, an empty car seat, and an emptiness in my heart. The dreams I had of holding my baby and watching him grow were gone. I wanted to shout, scream, cry. I wanted to blame someone, something. I wanted to hide under the covers and never come out. I was overwhelmed with the flood of emotions running through my veins—anger, sadness, depression, fear, guilt, despair. I had to walk into my home to see a nursery that would never be used. I had to unpack a chest full of baby clothes that would never be worn. I inhaled the scent of baby powder and baby lotion never to be applied.

I dropped into a deep depression. I wondered if my life mattered.

And yet, over time, the passing of my son helped me wake up to the truth of who I was, how I wanted to show up, and the legacy and impact I wanted to make on this planet while I was lucky enough to have a breath and a life to live.

How was I going to show up and honor who he was and what his life meant to me?

This question has led me on many paths. One of the first I pursued after my son's death was to serve an orphanage. When I reached out to an orphanage in Indonesia, they said that any money I donated would simply get taken in transit and asked if I instead could bring them supplies in person.

Within two weeks I had gathered hygiene kits, toothbrushes, soccer balls, clothes, and shoes and had secured a flight to Bali. This was the most last-minute thing I had ever done. But bringing supplies and visiting and playing with those kids filled me up with more than anything I ever gave. As I held them and they held me, I experienced a profound healing, the kind that allowed me to release the physicality of my son while holding on to the knowing he was with me in spirit every day, all day. I healed by giving to other children in his name. When I was in Bali, I made a commitment to myself that I would return with my family one day and serve more. I would show my children the power of service and leaving a legacy. I would teach them the impact we can have when we give to others and how, when we give to others, we also receive.

A few years later, I followed through on my promise. My family and I were on our way to Bali. We intended to live there for a few months and planned that every week we would visit a new orphanage and be of service. We got a local driver named Made.

When Made pulled up outside our first orphanage, he said, "I'll just wait here in the car until you are done."

Something inside me told me that he needed to join us. He needed to participate and serve alongside us. I was paying for his time, so he couldn't really get out of it when I insisted he come.

He stayed close to me. Despite the language barrier, Made and I had a deep understanding right off the bat. At one point I was holding a six-month-old boy who had tested positive for HIV. He had been left on the street. He was adorable, and I was just enraptured holding him. Made leaned over and asked me, "Why do you do this?"

I explained, "I lost my son a few years ago. The year after he passed, I came here to serve in his name, to heal my heart and do what I could with the means I was given. I wanted my family to experience it as well. I'm here because I want to be here. I want to give love, as much love as I can to these children while I'm living."

Made began to cry. He explained that about a year ago, he had lost his own two-year-old son. He said, "I've been so sad. We loved him so much and he's not here."

I looked at him. "This is why you are our driver. This is why you're sitting in this orphanage." I placed the baby in his arms, and with tears rolling down his cheeks, Made held him so tenderly, giving all the love he could to this little boy.

On that day and many days after, I witnessed my healing, my children's healing, Craig's healing, and Made's healing as we used pain as our fuel to serve.

ABUNDANCE ACTION

Legacy isn't something that has to wait until you have a certain amount in your bank account or until you have the perfect life or your ducks in a row. Legacy is a day-by-day opportunity to serve, show up for others, get out of your own way, and start to live a life outside of yourself.

Deep within our cells is a longing to use our genius, our resources, our love, and our lives to make a difference in someone else's. It takes courage to be kind. It takes courage to drop your idea of separation. It takes courage to stop being complicit with tasks, jobs, and people that are not kind, heart-centered, or making a positive impact. It takes courage to use all that is within you for a greater mission that will affect the world. Starting today, do one of these three things over the next few weeks:

1. Start putting aside 10 percent of your earnings (no matter how small or big that number is). Where could you donate resources for others?

2. Write down someone who could use some love today. Who will you anoint with your love? What could you say or do that would lift their spirits and remind them of *their* value and power?

3. Reach out to a nonprofit organization in your community that could use your expertise or your time and offer your services.

lessons from the ahu

What you think, you believe.
What you focus on, you attract.
What you do, you become.

As we took this journey together, walking through our stories, discovering our truths, and using the ahus as our guides and markers along the way, we have no doubt begun to live as the truest, most authentic versions of ourselves.

Just like the ahus on our path, we have harnessed these internal truths:

We are solid, not rigid. We are bending and swaying to the miracles of life. We are no longer rigid in trying to get others to see things the way we do, and we are flexible and curious in our beliefs.

We rise up. We rise above old, limiting beliefs. We stand tall. We use our truth and our voice for love. We own our path and mark it for others to learn from.

We are balanced. The key to an ahu's miraculous architecture is its ability to maintain balance. Even as it defies gravity, it holds its center. We too can defy all that would weigh us down by maintaining harmony in our lives, stacking ourselves atop eternal truths, and trusting in our internal guidance systems.

We are grounded. We plant our feet faithfully on the love and wisdom of Mother Earth. We use her as our guide to ultimate health and happiness.

We are aligned. We check in with our alignment by following our true north. We trust our gut instincts and adjust our thoughts, our beliefs, and our actions along the way.

When we fall, we rebuild. The winds of crisis or change will come. We are not afraid, nor do we fear hard work and grit. We rebuild over and over again. We never give up.

We guide others. We understand our life is not our own. When we do the work to heal old wounds, when we choose to love even if we are not loved, when we rewire our stories, light our internal torches, and build our dreams, we give others permission to do the same. We know our path shapes all the lives before us and the ones to come.

Let the lessons from the ahu

guide you on the path toward the river of abundance.

resources

*I've created some free guided resources for
your journey to abundance that you'll find referenced
throughout this book. You can access them all at
www.EmbraceAbundanceBook.com/resources.*

acknowledgments

When it comes to writing books, writing the acknowledgments is one of my greatest joys. Books are not born from the author alone; they're born from all the people, the moments, the experiences, and the essence of nature that the author was graced to walk through.

The first acknowledgment I want to make is to Mother Nature and the Source who loves all. Every day I walked among the trees, I stepped on her loving, steady soil, I felt her wind, and I felt the sun on my face as her wisdom seeped through me and into this book.

Second, I'd like to thank my family, Sarah, Samantha, and Craig. It is their love, their patience, that gives me wings to be in my soul's expression. I'm grateful for the Hay House family, for believing in me and allowing me to share my knowings and my gifts through their platform. Thank you to my editors. We were a triad of love and perseverance. And especially I'm grateful for each one of you, the ones who have read this book, the ones who have taken this time to grow, to evolve, and to understand that we all deserve abundance.

about the author

Danette May is the co-founder of Mindful Health and Earth Echo Foods. Millions of people worldwide have utilized her life-changing programs. Danette is a sought-after VIP coach for leaders and celebrities, renowned speaker, and best-selling author of such books as *The Rise*. Her motivational videos have over 500 million views across all her brands. She is on a mission to help individuals understand their unlimited potential and show up in their divine gifts.

Follow Danette for more inspiration:

Facebook: https://www.facebook.com/TheDanetteMay

Instagram: https://instagram.com/thedanettemay

YouTube: https://www.youtube.com/user/danettemay

Website: https://www.danettemay.com

Hay House Titles of Related Interest

YOU CAN HEAL YOUR LIFE, the movie,
starring Louise Hay & Friends
(available as a 1-DVD program, an expanded 2-DVD set,
and an online streaming video)
Learn more at www.hayhouse.com/louise-movie

THE SHIFT, the movie,
starring Dr. Wayne W. Dyer
(available as a 1-DVD program, an expanded 2-DVD set,
and an online streaming video)
Learn more at www.hayhouse.com/the-shift-movie

BLACK GIRL IN LOVE (WITH HERSELF): A Guide to Self-Love, Healing, and Creating the Life You Truly Deserve, by Trey Anthony

GOOD VIBES, GOOD LIFE: A Real-World Guide to Achieving a Greater Life, by Vex King

SH#T YOUR EGO SAYS: Strategies to Overthrow Your Ego and Become the Hero of Your Story, by James McCrae

SUPER ATTRACTOR: Methods for Manifesting a Life Beyond Your Wildest Dreams, by Gabrielle Bernstein

All of the above are available at your local bookstore,
or may be ordered by contacting Hay House (see next page).

We hope you enjoyed this Hay House book. If you'd like to receive our online catalog featuring additional information on Hay House books and products, or if you'd like to find out more about the Hay Foundation, please contact:

Hay House, Inc., P.O. Box 5100, Carlsbad, CA 92018-5100
(760) 431-7695 or (800) 654-5126
(760) 431-6948 (fax) or (800) 650-5115 (fax)
www.hayhouse.com® • www.hayfoundation.org

———

Published in Australia by: Hay House Australia Pty. Ltd.,
18/36 Ralph St., Alexandria NSW 2015
Phone: 612-9669-4299 • *Fax:* 612-9669-4144
www.hayhouse.com.au

Published in the United Kingdom by: Hay House UK, Ltd.,
The Sixth Floor, Watson House, 54 Baker Street, London W1U 7BU
Phone: +44 (0)20 3927 7290 • *Fax:* +44 (0)20 3927 7291
www.hayhouse.co.uk

Published in India by: Hay House Publishers India,
Muskaan Complex, Plot No. 3, B-2, Vasant Kunj, New Delhi 110 070
Phone: 91-11-4176-1620 • *Fax:* 91-11-4176-1630
www.hayhouse.co.in

———

Access New Knowledge.
Anytime. Anywhere.

Learn and evolve at your own pace
with the world's leading experts.

www.hayhouseU.com